6/13

D0175290

TO EAT

TO EAT

A COUNTRY LIFE

JOE ECK *and*

WAYNE WINTERROWD

Illustrations by Bobbi Angell

With recipes by Beatrice Tosti di Valminuta

FARRAR, STRAUS AND GIROUX   NEW YORK

Farrar, Straus and Giroux
18 West 18th Street, New York 10011

Grateful acknowledgment is made for permission to reprint "Pea Season" from
Our Life in Gardens by Joe Eck and Wayne Winterrowd. Copyright © 2009
by Joe Eck and Wayne Winterrowd. Reprinted by permission
of Farrar, Straus and Giroux, LLC.

Library of Congress Cataloging-in-Publication Data
Eck, Joe.
    To eat : a country life / Joe Eck and Wayne Winterrowd ; illustrations
by Bobbi Angell ; with recipes by Beatrice Tosti di Valminuta. — 1st ed.
        p.   cm.
    Includes index.
    ISBN 978-0-374-27832-8 (alk. paper)
        1. Vegetable gardening.   2. Domestic animals.   3. Farm life.
    I. Winterrowd, Wayne.   II. Title.

SB320.9.E25 2013
635—dc23

                                                                    2012048074

Designed by Jonathan D. Lippincott

www.fsgbooks.com
www.twitter.com/fsgbooks • www.facebook.com/fsgbooks

1   3   5   7   9   10   8   6   4   2

For our son, Fotios Bouzikos

EPIGRAM TO A FRIEND AND SON:

Son, and my friend, I had not called you so
To me, or been the same to you, if show,
Profit, or chance had made us; but I know
What, by that name, we each to other owe,
Freedom and truth; with love from those begot;
Wise crafts, on which the flatterer ventures not.
                                        —Ben Jonson

Contents

Preface: To Begin

by Joe Eck

This book was begun in 2010. It treats of one of the singular passions of our common life. Those passions have been many: art, gardening, music, and also eating. Eating has always been central. Every day for forty-two years, Wayne labored in the kitchen preparing a fine dinner. Almost the first question we discussed each morning was what we would eat that night. And in most of the year the answer lay in the vegetable garden. We said always that when age and infirmity came upon us, we would cling to that garden above all else. And it was always our favorite place to be, for there we were alone, far from the phone and the world.

Wayne died on September 17, 2010, so this will be the last book under our common name. But the vegetable garden will still be planted each spring, now by me alone. Of course I still need to eat, and well, but also in homage to a long life together. The Greeks believed that one lived so long as any person had knowledge of you, of your face, your voice, and your work. This book is our work. May it give pleasure.

TO EAT

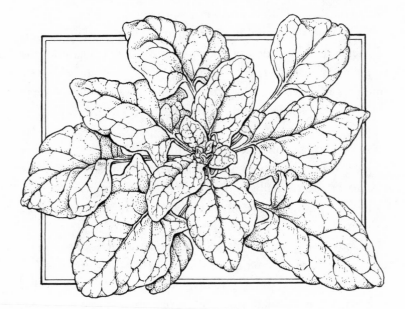

THE JOURNEY

In the very early days of our life together and our gardening experience, it seems that much good came to us from the houses we rented. We left our rural life in Pepperell, Massachusetts, in 1972 to spend a glorious year in Copenhagen on Fulbright appointments to the University of Copenhagen and at the Folk University. Though the city was rich in cultural experiences—the Danish Royal Opera and Ballet, the fine old architecture, fascinating museums, historic castles, excellent restaurants—our life there offered little to us as gardeners. The apartment we succeeded in renting (with great difficulty, as we were transient) was spacious and well lit, on the third floor of a rather anonymous modern building with no land, though there was a splendid view from our living room window of the Spanish embassy, with a great flowering chestnut tree in front and a pretty formal reception garden behind. We made up for our lack, as we had before on Beacon Street in Boston, with cut flowers.

Through the incredibly mandarin but somehow startlingly efficient social system of Copenhagen ("My cousin knows someone who is related to someone in the Bureau of . . . I'll make a call"), we quickly secured a quite illegitimate license to shop the wholesale flower market early in the morning, and we would return with sheaves of improbable blossoms for vases—proteras and gladioli, camellias and forced branches of quince—and often with potted flowering plants—*Cinerarias*, *Cyclamen*, forced bulbs and *Kalanchoes*—which gave us about as much pleasure as the flowers in vases and then were for the dustbin.

Doing without, in most human passions, can lead to a powerful urge to recover what is missing. So when we returned to Boston a year later, though we savored our renewed love for that old city, we immediately secured a plot in its famous Victory Gardens in the Fenway, bordering the aptly named Muddy River. We were urban dwellers still, but we had a scrap of ground we could cultivate on fine spring mornings and radishes we could harvest hardly a month after. We had sunlight, too, which we had not seen for all our autumn and winter in Copenhagen, and the crunch of a really fresh bean, which we had missed since leaving Pepperell two years before.

Everyone we knew in the Victory Gardens was more or less mad with desire. Our neighbors were an assorted lot—a furniture salesman, a stylish young couple in real estate, two elderly spinsters of reduced means, a leather-clad man who drove a motorcycle, an aristocratic lady of German origin—but we all shared one common passion: the need to dig in the dirt and raise something. But we left the Fenway after two years and moved to a rented house in Whitingham, Vermont, while we waited to find a house of our own.

We lived there for two more years, and it was a good house,

old but not much remodeled over its many years. There were some original features, beamed ceilings, a splendid fireplace, and a large glassed-in south-facing porch, the "drying porch" of old Vermont houses where winter laundry was hung and where we built staging and had wonderful flowering plants throughout the winter. There was a pleasant sunlit 1950s Betty Crocker kitchen, with a table in the middle where for once, never before or after, we used a tablecloth.

But, as before, in Pepperell, the real treasures of the property were ample land, woods, and a fine barn in which we could keep chickens and other poultry. From the land, which was ancient, well-tended pasture when we came, we fashioned an enormous vegetable garden, really enough to feed a family of twelve. But we were hungry, not just for vegetables but also for plenitude, and for the joys of the work itself. In some ways, that was the most productive vegetable garden we ever had, in part because of the virgin nature of the soil, and in part because our little plot in the Victory Gardens had allowed our passions to leak out in a trickle but not in the flood we wanted. We grew everything, and we froze food then (we do not now). We can vividly remember the day that eighteen heads of cauliflower came ripe all at once and had to be processed and frozen the night before an early departure for a family wedding.

Most vividly, we remember the spinach we grew. Spinach can be a cranky crop, demanding cool weather, full sun, lots of moisture, perfect drainage, and deep, rich, fertile earth, with a neutral soil reading, somewhere close on either side of 6.0. We did not know much of that then. So, with beginner's luck, we appeared to happen on just the right combination, and our spinach was huge, with leaves dark and richly crinkled, on heads that were fully a foot across. Distant memory can become gilded, but it seems to us that we picked spinach from late May all the way to July, and we never remember any that was stunted or bolted or yellow or had aphids.

That is not the first experience that has given us the sense that the heavens smile on novice gardeners who have little but borrowed knowledge and their own intense enthusiasm. We have never grown such good spinach since, and certainly not in our present garden, the one we will have until we die. Contiguous both to our poultry house and our pig house, and not far from our cow pasture, it is unusually well endowed with well-rotted compost, both autumn and spring. An extensive underground drainage system gives us some rows that can be readied just at the proverbial point at which the frost leaves the ground and the soil is workable. That is actually perhaps a month or even six weeks before the last frost, but spinach, with several other crops, will germinate in cold soil and is resistant to light frost. So the day we plant spinach, along with broad beans, onions, and leeks, is a joyful day.

If we have been diligent the autumn before, rows have already been turned up to receive the great benefits of winter, which improves their tilth. Still in spring they must be composted and turned again, and then smoothed down with the back of a rake to receive the seed. There is pleasure in the work itself, and a challenge, for one must try to make the bed perfectly. And then the seed is put in. Broad beans are easy, for their flattened, thumb-sized seeds can be as neatly arrayed as a column of marching soldiers, and then gently pressed into the soft earth, preferably eye side down, so the first questing root will go in the right direction without having to wiggle itself around.

Other crops join the spinach and broad beans in this first working of the garden in springtime. Though it will be yet two weeks before we sow the peas, now in earliest April we can plant onions and leeks, arugula and mâche, and radishes. There is pleasure in anticipating the early harvest this labor will yield. But the great pleasure is the earth in our hands, connected to it again after a long winter's absence.

APPLES

In forty-one years of gardening, not every day gets remembered. Still, we remember quite a few: the day we planted the yew hedge, the day we laid the first stones of the wall that would surround the perennial garden, our first harvest of strawberries. One in particular stands out: the day we planted the apples. The land was new to us and apple trees had always figured large in our fantasy of rural life. And unlike soft fruits, such as strawberries and raspberries, they took years to develop and to bear and so we were eager to begin. We knew enough to want antiques, though we weren't quite sure what that meant. And as we planned on planting but four, the varieties we chose seemed particularly significant. Of course we were planting whips, baby trees the thickness of a pencil, hard to picture a fruiting size in our lifetimes.

Of the four we chose, one, Yellow Transparent, dates from 1870 and was imported from Russia for its superior hardiness. It has pale golden skin and bears very early, often by mid-August. And that was for us a particular recommendation since each August a young man, Jacob Lifson, the son of one of our oldest and dearest friends, spent some weeks with us in a place as removed from his real home, Los Angeles, as could be conceived. Jacob was terribly fond of apple pie, and as it happens Yellow Transparent from mid-August on bears abundant fruit out of which fine pies can be made. It has always here been called simply Jacob's tree.

From the first, we saw this place as part of a continuum of New England life, a place that honors the old ways and continues onward with them. So the house we built is a classic center-chimney Cape with steep roofs and small-paned windows. The barn is a classic L, piled high with hay and farm tools, including a fine nineteenth-century scythe that the very modern young man who works with us insists on using to cut the meadow. An apple only a hundred and forty years old didn't seem ideal, however much pleasure it gave to Jacob, so next to it we planted Summer Rambo—or more elegantly named Rambour Franc—known to have originated near Amiens, France. It is on the earliest list of apples grown on this continent by the first European colonists. That, plus the fact that it is disease resistant, vigorous, ripens in early September, and possesses an acid but richly fragrant flesh made it settle more appropriately into our little collection.

Our intention was to plant four trees to form the eastern boundary of our new vegetable garden. It, like the infant apples, was but a garden of the mind with no proper paths, established asparagus, strawberry beds, and a stone wall but just begun, which would take four years to complete. And now over thirty years later, the wall done, the paths settled, and the little apple seedlings grown to gnarly trees with twelve-inch-diameter trunks, I am still not sure that we take more pleasure in its present incarnation than we took in its first making.

The third tree yet to plant was simply common if ancient. Discovered in 1811 by John McIntosh on his farm near the Saint Lawrence River, it had by the late 1960s become the most commercially common apple. It is crisp and sharp, vigorous and hardy, and ripens well after Summer Rambo and Yellow Transparent. But it must be sprayed with pesticides and in any case is available in every market from farm stand to super. Were we to choose again, a dozen others, Spitzenburg, Thomas Jefferson's favorite, or perhaps Roxbury Russet, grown since the early 1600s, or many others, would hold that place. But the tree is healthy and well formed, the taste is familiar from our childhood, and it makes an excellent sauce.

We did best, though, with the fourth tree in the quartet, for it is generally thought of as the finest of all dessert apples. Cox's Orange Pippen ripens late for us, not before early October, but it keeps quite well and a box of them rests just out the back door most of the autumn. It is wonderful eaten out of hand, as sauce, and certainly as pies. We are hardly alone in feeling that if we could have but one apple, Cox would be it. So vigorous a tree is it that we have allowed a *Rosa canina* to scramble through it largely for the abundant large red hips that spangle the rose and hence the tree each fall.

This quartet of apple trees, near sticks when planted in 1978, seem ancient now and form the eastern boundary of what has become our perennial garden, the only truly formal room in the garden.

But for one. The vegetable garden, too, is a formal space of squares and rectangles, straight paths, and fixed vistas. And we grow apples there, too, but in a very different way. Many years ago our good friends Michèle and Jean-Claude La Montagne took us to a festive garden fair held each October at the Domaine de Courson, a splendid château about thirty miles outside of Paris. It was a day of extraordinary sights, great delight, and improvident purchases. But the strongest impression made on us was a hedge of free-standing espaliered apples, more than a century old. Like so many effects first seen in the gardens of others, it was one we were determined to copy. And so our own little potager is bisected by four apple espaliers freestanding and only thirty years of age, not centuries. Yet they are already a beauty in themselves and a recollection of a memorable day spent in the company of memorable friends.

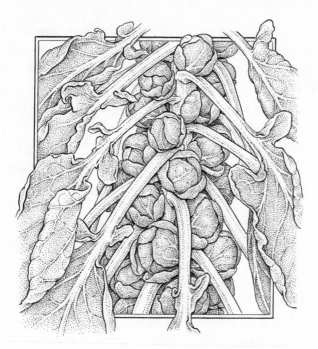

BRUSSELS SPROUTS

In a lifetime of gardening there is little we haven't grown, much of it fairly well. Gardening is our passion and our trade. We lecture on it, write about it, and generally pass for experts. Yet there seem always to be plants that everyone else grows with great ease but that fail for us. So it was for many years with spinach, a crop of which we grew splendidly on our first attempt and each year thereafter failed at utterly. Not until our friend Jack Manix told us that spinach requires a really sweet soil and prefers dry conditions to wet did we again manage to produce a respectable crop.

That sadly was also true of brassicas—broccoli, cauliflower, cabbage and, most painfully, Brussels sprouts. Initial splendid success was followed by year after year of ever greater failure. The cause eventually became apparent—our soil had come to be infested with a particularly nasty fungus, *Plasmodiophora bras-sicae*, commonly called clubroot. The first symptom of the disease is the wilting of foliage on sunny days followed by stunted growth. Should you pull the plant from the earth, you will find that the roots are swollen and misshapen. Any plant so infected will shortly perish—but not that plant alone, for the disease is virulent and will quickly take off the entire crop. Plants other than brassicas can also be infected, most sinisterly a weed common in all our gardens, *Barbarea vulgaris*, St. Barbara's weed, which will quickly spread the disease throughout the garden. And once the soil is infected, it remains so for as long as ten years, and no brassica, not broccoli or cabbage, cauliflower or Brussels sprouts, can be grown there.

When this disease first came upon us five or six years after we established the present vegetable garden, we fought it. We moved all the brassicas as far from last year's plot as the dimensions of the garden allowed. We limed, for we had learned that the fungus particularly thrived in acid soils. We eliminated cauliflower, as it seemed most susceptible to infection. But then we gave up cabbage and even broccoli, a vegetable we are both deeply fond of. Still we held tenaciously to Brussels sprouts though they grew less and less well until eventually our harvest more resembled a mess of peas than a bowl of sprouts.

And then we mourned; there was so much about them that we loved. The way they looked, little tiny cabbages arrayed up and down a gawky stalk with a broad hat of cabbage leaves on top. The way real ones taste, that is, those that have endured more than a touch of frost and so are sweet, unrecognizable compared to the great green globes grown in California and sold in even northern markets. We sometimes simply boil them and dress them with butter or, more often, turn them in butter in a skillet till almost black and sometimes with our own bacon folded in. And even cold while standing over the kitchen sink of a morning waiting for the coffee to brew. But we most missed their harvest, always in November or December, tearing them free from their frozen stalks with our frozen fingers while the real first snows of winter blew around us.

And then we learned again how to succeed with them. We had for years been adding copious quantities of compost taken from the pig house liberally laced with pine shavings. And though we had been liming the rows, it had been by handfuls, when what was needed were buckets. And all around us were midden heaps of compost, cow and chicken, duck and goose aged two years and free of pine shavings. Lime, too, was cheap, and fifty-pound bags were not heavy for John Thayer to carry up the steep five-hundred-foot-long path to the vegetable garden.

Where potatoes had grown last year and corn the year before, we planted Brussels sprouts. They did not wilt in the sun and grew so tall they bent themselves to earth with the weight of their fruit. And today, December 6, we brought perhaps sixty stalks to the keeping room, enough to last the winter.

Hashed Brussels Sprouts
First served to us by an old friend in Kentucky, this method glorifies broccoli as well.

Using a most sharp knife, slice the sprouts into small slivers. Sauté them in lots of butter. Add cream if you like. Not healthy, but delicious.

CABBAGE

Nineteen seventy-two was not a happy time. We had fled to Europe, fled from an America that shamed us and frightened us. War was all about us and we were not willing. But even in the safety of Europe, it came. We were sitting in a London restaurant at Christmas and Nixon's bombing of Cambodia was suddenly the talk at every table. Grief was all any of us could feel.

Put against that the next night and you know the triviality of humans. For the next night we went to Simpson's-in-the-Strand, one of the oldest restaurants in London, begun in 1828 and a palace of pleasure. We still feel guilty at the comfort we took there. But that is what British food is. It is comfort. And we had that night the most comforting dish, cabbage in a napkin. A linen napkin, to be discarded at the end.

We were in a grand dining room, oak paneled with gracious

waiters in livery. This was England and we would have beef and whatever else came with it.

And that, to our startlement, was cabbage in a napkin. So simple. Just a cabbage, steamed all day, wrapped in a fine linen napkin. What does that do? It drives off the sulfur. Why does British food have such a nasty reputation? It often is good in its simple way, good joints, steamed vegetables, fine pudding. The very essence of one of the finest eateries in the world, Chez Panisse: so simple, just splendid goods treated with respect.

Cabbage is a common thing, easy to grow, forthright in its flavor and texture, sturdy, and with us all the winter long. It will grow in summer, but in summer there are so many things to eat: beans, corn, tomatoes, squash. We save cabbage for autumn and winter, sowing in July, planting out in August, harvesting in October and November.

And what do we do with it? At the first just a salad, shredded and dressed, a summer salad prolonged into autumn. Then in Japanese soups served in bowls made from our own maples by our friend Peter Wimmelman, an old Vermonter steeped in the craft of wood in the forest. Then in stir-fries with our own pork, then stuffed in the Polish fashion, a deep winter dish, rich, hardy, caloric.

And what do we grow? Firm headed, sometimes in queer shapes, arrow headed, or tiny just for fun. But we also grow Savoy, a much less tight-headed form with corrugated loose heads and delectable texture particularly good for stuffing.

And red ones. Ruby Perfection for early, Integro for late, both treasured by German palates. Sometimes with apples or pears, half sweet, half savory.

Cabbage has cousins, many: Brussels sprouts, kohlrabi, cauliflower, and broccoli. We grow them all, but broccoli is the best. One particular broccoli, Romanesco, glimpsed first in the Campo dei Fiori in Rome, Madonna's breast. Delectable, smooth, buttery. It is for autumn, for it will not abide heat. But planted in August, it brings to October the excitement of July, peas, or of August, corn. Its form is Dadaesque—great green aggressive cones, demanding attention and repaying with deliciousness. Eating is deeply sexual. With Romanesco that is blushingly at the surface.

We misuse our food. We treat it as a mere necessity when it is in fact an enormous pleasure. To continue the sexual analogy, it is like to treating sex as a duty to get children when of course it is a deep gratification in itself. It is remarkable how the Puritan inheritance still colors our mental life. Our food is nothing fancy. Always brief in the cooking and the eating. Get it over with, it is just sustenance. But of course we don't really believe this. We resist this Puritan ideal, left over. A simple cabbage or broccoli or cauliflower is, however you prepare it, goodness and pleasure, and what else ought we to seek in our lives?

Cavolo Romanesco con Acciughe
(Roman Cauliflower with Anchovies)
I am not supposed to eat too many brassicas, but I am shameless when confronted with a Romanesco cauliflower. I can eat tons of it.

4 tablespoons extra-virgin olive oil
5 cloves garlic, cut in thick slices
4 anchovies in salt, washed, boned, and chopped (you
 can also use good quality anchovies packed in oil)
Pinch chili (peperoncino) flakes
2 pounds *Cavolo romanesco*, trimmed and ready to be
 cooked

Allow me a few words on anchovies. Why do most people in the United States hate anchovies? We seem to have no problem eating Thai or Vietnamese food seasoned with abundant fish sauce. And what do you think fish sauce is? Ambrosia? No, it is some sort of juice from dried, salted, and possibly fermented fish, if not anchovies then a very close relative. I use anchovies in everything and I do not say it to anybody. It makes food sing.

In a frying pan over low heat, sauté the olive oil, garlic, anchovies, and chili flakes. Use a wooden spoon to mash and melt the anchovies. Add the Romanesco florets and cook over low heat, covered, until it looks like a mash, about 30 minutes. Taste for seasoning—we do not add salt because of the anchovies—and adjust to your liking.

SERVES 4
From the kitchen of Beatrice Tosti di Valminuta

Cavolo Verza Strascinato
("Dragged" Savoy Cabbage)
I love cabbage, especially Savoy, and this easy dish will convert many cabbage haters to fans. This is a wonderful side for pork and beef or can be enjoyed with eggs or on its own. It keeps well in the refrigerator and is a delicious leftover.

1 head Savoy cabbage (or any cabbage you fancy)
4 tablespoons extra-virgin olive oil
Pinch spicy crushed chili pepper of your liking (you can omit this if you do not enjoy the heat)
1 large onion, sliced
Sea salt to taste
1 bay leaf
1 tablespoon red wine vinegar

Cut the cabbage in half and in quarters, and slice in ¼-inch ribbons.

In a frying pan over medium heat, heat the olive oil until it is hot. Add the chili flakes, onion, cabbage, sea salt, and bay leaf.

Give it a stir and cover. I like the cabbage to reach a blondish cara-
mel color before I stir again. Reduce the heat to low and cook for
15 to 20 minutes. When the cabbage is reaching the cooking
point, add the vinegar and stir. Taste for seasoning and adjust if
you need to.

SERVES 4

From the kitchen of Beatrice Tosti di Valminuta

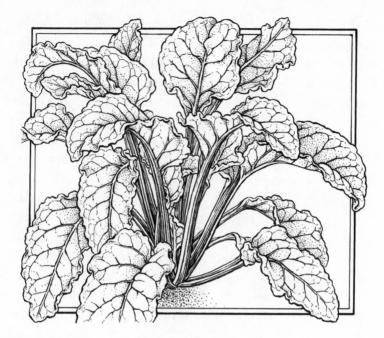

CHARD

Chard is a kind of beet, botanically identical to *Beta vulgaris*, though it belongs to a separate group. Chard possesses almost all the virtues one could ask for in a vegetable. It is rich in vitamins and minerals, productive over a long period from one sowing, and tolerant of a wide variety of climate and soil conditions. It will accept some shade and is even indifferent to light frosts. It is also very beautiful, with thick stems of green, ruby red, yellow, orange, or white, according to variety (Rainbow chard is a mix of all colors), surrounded by huge shiny, crinkled leaves of dark spinach green. Grown well, it is a stately plant, reaching perhaps three feet in height. It is so handsome that it frequently appears as accent points in mixed planting of annuals and perennials, and even as single specimens in containers.

For all its virtues, we always plant a row of chard. But we must admit that we neglect it in our kitchen. It is the good child that goes unnoticed, for at any point that it is harvestable—which is to say from tiny thinnings one may add to salads to giant leaves touched by October frost—there is almost always something in the garden we would rather eat, perhaps because, unlike chard, that something is transitory. For example, it is often said that chard may be eaten "like spinach." But in the brief season spinach is at its prime, who would want a substitute? Though a few tender leaves of chard might be tossed into a mixed salad in late June for color and variety, lettuce is queen of salads, and the many colors and forms in which we grow it seem to provide variety enough. In high summer, there is corn, and beans, broccoli, and tomatoes and, briefly, artichokes. And in autumn, there are all the root vegetables—beets and carrots, celeriac and new potatoes. Even in late autumn, when supplies in the vegetable garden begin to thin out, there are Brussels sprouts, the eagerly awaited last fine thing of the season. So, though mature, frosted chard is superb sautéed in good olive oil and plenty of garlic (the cloves left whole, a vegetable in themselves), our plants—certainly much admired for their beauty and the air of perfect good health they carry—tend to stand unused.

With one exception. We live in an Italian village, heavily populated by immigrants from Trentino, Alto Adige, the northernmost province of Italy, hard up against the Austrian border. They came to Readsboro in large numbers to work in five huge furniture factories located here, the last of which, a great red abandoned wooden hulk on the northern edge of the town, was torn down only fifteen years ago. But their descendants have remained, and so in the old cemeteries near the gravestones of Spragues and Pratts, Birches and Boyds, you will see the names Comai, Marchegiani, Bolognani, Codogni, and Scaia. Their descendants are now third- or fourth-generation Americans, but they have preserved many of the cooking traditions their great-grandparents brought with them, such as rabbit or game cooked for half a day in a rich tomato sauce with rosemary and served with polenta. We also know that grappa is still made in this town in somebody's basement. Our friendly plumber gave us some in a plastic jug, and it was excellent, though our request to buy more was met with stony silence.

Of all the dishes particular to this village, *caponetti* is perhaps the best. It is feast food, since there is no reason even to begin it unless you make fifty or a hundred bundles. It consists essentially of a rich stuffing, made with good bread and sautéed onion, garlic, celery, and some parsley, moistened with strong chicken stock and a beaten egg, much as one would make stuffing for a Thanksgiving turkey. But to the mix is added grated Parmesan cheese, some olive oil, and plenty of blanched chard, squeezed dry and shredded. Place a generous tablespoon of the mix in the center of a large blanched grape leaf, and fold over the lobes of the leaf and roll it up to make a tidy bundle. Then tie it with clean kitchen string. Keep the water in which the grape leaves were blanched (about 3 or 4 quarts) at a vigorous boil, and slip in 6 or 7 *caponetti* at a time to poach for about 10 minutes. Remove them with a slotted spoon to drain in a colander, and cook 6 or 7 more, until the whole batch is done. Heap the *caponetti* on a large platter lined with fresh grape leaves, with slices of lemon and lime scattered among them, and serve tepid or even cold. Each diner removes the strings of his or her bundle, opens out the grape leaf, squeezes a lemon or lime slice over it, and dribbles on a bit of good olive oil. The grape leaf is not eaten, though it is hardly mere garnish, since it contributes its own subtle acidic taste to the contents within.

Ideally, *caponetti* should be eaten outdoors, preferably under a grape arbor. These also exist in our town, and there is one in our garden. What we cannot seem to get hold of is the grappa, or anyone to teach us how to make it. The blunt fact is that we have lived here only thirty-five years, and that is not enough to get the recipe. So we must be grateful for *caponetti*, which are really superb. One is grateful for the good things that are freely offered; for the rest, one must patiently wait.

Passato di Verdure
(Vegetable Soup)

This is my all-time favorite soup. You can use any green vegetables you want—string beans, asparagus, broccoli, zucchini, watercress, escarole . . . My ingredients change with the season, and I serve it hot or cold. I always generously drizzle with extra-virgin olive oil.

½ cup extra-virgin olive oil
2 carrots, coarsely chopped
1 onion, coarsely chopped
5 shallots, coarsely chopped
5 cloves garlic
1 heart celery (white part only), coarsely chopped
1 bunch swiss chard, washed and shredded with your
    hands
1 bunch spinach, washed and shredded
1 bunch kale or Tuscan kale (depending on the season),
    washed and shredded, with stalks removed
3 tablespoons (at least) sea salt
Some spicy pepper if you like the heat

You will need an immersion blender.

Place your heaviest stockpot on the stove over high heat. I use my earthenware pot from Italy. Add the oil, the chopped vegetables and all the greens, the salt, and the chili pepper. Cover with water. Bring to a boil, lower the heat to low, cover, and let cook for 1 to 1½ hours. No, you do not need to sauté anything; all the vegetables and the greens go at the same time. They used to cook this soup on the side of the fire and it would cook all day.

Taste for seasoning, remove the soup from the heat and turn it into a *passato* (mash) using your immersion blender. (*Passato* comes from *passaverdure*, the hand-churned vegetable mill that was used until not too long ago. I still use mine every day to prepare potatoes for the gnocchi we serve at Il Bagatto.) You can add cooked rice to the soup, or bread, poached eggs, pasta, or broken spaghetti. It freezes well and is so good for you.

SERVES 6–8
From the kitchen of Beatrice Tosti di Valminuta

FOOD FOR THOUGHT

I am an avid consumer of vegetables. When I visit North Hill in the summer, I can be found at 7:30 in the morning standing in the vegetable garden munching on morning-dew-fresh chicory, tomatoes, and blueberries. I am also a big fan of cooked vegetables. It is true indeed that raw vegetables have more nutrients, but it is also true that our body has an easier time absorbing nutrients from cooked vegetables.

A study shows that we absorb more beta-carotene from a cooked carrot than from a raw one even though the raw carrot has a higher content of beta-carotene.

CHICORY

One can hardly call January 8 autumn. But here we are in this warming world only now potting the Whitloof. In years past they would have been dug and potted by Thanksgiving, but as the world has warmed, they live longer in the earth each year. We dig them at the last possible moment, just as the ground freezes solid till springtime. Long, dark roots like some primitive carrot, they are in fact chicory, beloved by the Italians, who have multiplied its forms into hundreds of shapes and uses. Most are eaten in salads or sautéed or in soups. But one, Whitloof, is for winter. It was in fact developed in Belgium—which is why it is also called Belgian endive—and introduced about 1870.

You sow it in spring, not too thickly, and then ignore it. It grows and in late autumn it dies back to its crown. Then you dig it.

Pot the roots, packed rather tightly together in sand or soil up to the crown. Then place perhaps six inches of peat over the crown, water the whole thing, put it in a dark place, and forget about it.

We make up several pots, the first put in warmth, the others in cold corners of the potting shed.

In about five weeks' time, that first pot shows green above the peat and we know it's time to harvest. Digging down through the peat, we cut the Whitloof just above the crown. What gets pulled from the peat cover is one of those firm, tight white Whitloofs, crisp and slightly bitter and, on a cold February day, something of a miracle. Miraculous in part because anyone can do this. No greenhouse is required, only a dark cool place, a garage or a closet or in a cellar. In the market their cost is $6 per pound. These are essentially free. And from a single twenty-foot row one has salads till May. Wayne and I have pursued self-sufficiency with a kind of fervor all our lives. Our first book on vegetables is called *Living Seasonally* and is a manifesto for eating only what oneself produces in its season. Nothing comes closer to this ideal than Whitloof.

Its cousin radicchio is more honestly an autumn crop. It cannot be forced and must be eaten fresh from the garden in its time, usually from August till late October. It is tolerant of hard frost, down to 20 degrees or so, but lower than that it rots. It presents two quite distinct shapes, tight and round rather like iceberg lettuce and tall and sharply arrow shaped. The latter is used, at least at North Hill, for grilling. There are several that we grow. Rossa di Treviso must experience cold weather to color properly, that is, a rich ruby with pure white ribs. Though its form is a bit lax, it is a reliable performer in our garden. On many an autumn night we take chops from our own recently slaughtered pigs and grill them with the radicchio over a wood fire. Dressed with a little olive oil, they offer a fine contrast to the Brussels sprouts and beets that constitute our usual autumn fare. Lately, for reasons of sheer snobbery, we have begun to grow Treviso Tardiva. It matures late, but really it seems not much later than the others though it is somewhat crankier to grow. The snob part is that it is the first Italian vegetable to be granted D.O.P. status by the EU just like champagne.

Anything from Treviso is especially prized here at North Hill, for as mentioned before, our village is half made of immigrants from Trentino. One of the great pleasures of living here has, from the first, been this vital link to northern Italian culture. Here we all cook good Italian food, and there is much toing and froing among us all to that wonderful world. In some ways our little village of Readsboro seems as real to us as our beloved East Village in New York City.

The other radicchios we grow are the round ones. Again the colors are usually a rich red, and our favorite, Palla Rossa, has perhaps the finest color in the genus. Happily it is easy to grow and consistently forms fine firm heads. Radicchio di Chioggia is very easy. Its color is paler than Palla Rossa. And most striking is Variegato di Castelfranco, which is red and light green more or less evenly marked all over. These radicchios are for us always salads, sometimes torn apart but often just halved or quartered and tossed with vinegar and oil. Always a bit bitter, they are a welcome tonic with which to face the coming winter.

Many years ago, our dear friend Guy Woolf, the celebrated potter, presented us with four blanching pots, made to historic patterns but as always informed with his own particular eccentricities. Tall, near two feet, with little removable lids to admit light to the blanching vegetable within, they might be used for rhubarb or kale, but we use ours for frisée. Not the Whitloof with which the chapter began, but the French frisée, also a chicory celebrated for its pale white heart. One knows it from every French bistro on earth. Always served with bacon and croutons.

Home gardeners are often frustrated when they fail to achieve that delicate yellow center, when it stays stubbornly green. But the trick is a blanching pot placed over the chicory about ten days before harvest. The outer green leaves are gathered tightly about the center, the pot is set, and its little lid removed. Just enough light reaches the plant to keep it healthy and at the same time so little light as to blanch out the center. Ten days later, the pot removed, the frisée is fine, white, tender, and delicious, which is our point. Gardening, good gardening, is an art, and like all the arts, it requires its instruments. Get thee to Guy's.

ONIONS

Onions are magical things, and the fact that they are work-horses in the kitchen takes no more away from their splendor than plowing a field does from a fine pair of Morgan horses. They are beautiful at every stage of their life, from tiny wisps of seedlings or newly sprouted sets through their growing season, when tubular leaves stand sturdily in rows, to their fine, silky skins when they are dried and put away for storage. Beauty in a vegetable ought to be reason enough to grow it, as it is with flowers. But onions have enormous utility as well, and so it is surprising that some vegetable garden writers, even quite good ones, sweep over them in dismissal.

Here, for example, is Christopher Lloyd, from his otherwise very fine book, *Gardener Cook* (Willow Creek Press, Minocqua, Wisconsin). "I see little point in the home-grown onion. Those on sale are as good and may have better keeping qualities, having been grown where summers are warm and more ripening. Your own crop is expected to last six or nine months . . . Buying them, 2lb at a time, they will have little scope for rotting." And here is Thalassa Cruso, whose 1975 *Making Vegetables Grow* was the first vegetable-gardening book we ever read and is still a sound tutor in many ways. "In small plots, growing onions to maturity takes time and much-needed space for a vegetable that does not taste all that different from the commercial product." It is highly unlikely that Christopher Lloyd ever read Ms. Cruso, but both make the same point: with onions, why bother?

We have many answers to this question, and were Christo still alive, we would enjoy taking on a good argument with him, for a sassy give-and-take was always one of the greatest pleasures of our conversations with him. Our first answer is one we have made throughout this book. No matter how excellent your local farm stand or how good the produce of your best local supermarket may be, there is something deeply rewarding to growing your own food, most especially when it can be harvested and kept alive through a long winter. For in that lie the elemental pleasures of security, so fragile to our forebears, when a larder of salted and pickled meats and a cold cellar full of apples and vegetables meant freedom from want, and a season of bad weather or diseases in the stock meant bitter hunger. A heap of silken-skinned onions curing in the sun calls back that atavistic memory, and here, we welcome it.

But is the supermarket onion as good or so nearly as good as to justify not growing one's own onions at all? It depends on the onion. In our garden, we grow onions for two purposes: to eat raw in various stages throughout the summer and into autumn, and for storage during the winter. The first raw onions we eat are Egyptian ones, hardy through our long winter and early to sprout in spring. They are discussed later in this book. But when they begin to make their curious heads of bulbils, they become rank and bitter, no longer fit for the table. They are followed then by immature bulbing onions, scallions, and we plant our young seedlings deliberately close together—as close as an inch apart—with the expectation of pulling every other one for the table, and then every other one, until they stand about five inches one from the other. Then they are left to swell their roots into proper onions.

Over the years, we have experimented with many forms of bunching onions, grown not for their bulbs but for their capacity to divide and redivide into scallions, much in the manner of chives. The idea of a crop that renews itself automatically—dig the clump, take half, plant back the rest—is very appealing, and indeed there is one very venerable clump that has survived from an early experiment with these onions, we think the Japanese variety called Ishikura. It stands square in the middle of one of the front paths, piercing through the straw, and there are strict instructions not to move it despite the inconvenience of its place-ment, because it is in a sense archival. Because it has never been divided, it has remained one sturdy clump of perhaps twenty stems. Early in July, it produces beautiful chartreuse-yellow puffs of flower among its hollow leaves, and when they ripen into seed, we always mean to take a dishful and sow them in a row. But in that busy season we miss our moment, and the seed dis-perses. So we rely on thinnings for our green onions.

For fully developed onions from the summer garden, we have tried many varieties, and we have come to feel that Ailsa Craig is the absolute best. Grown in ideal soil—fertile, with trace elements and rich in organic matter, in full sun with perfect drainage but plenty of moisture—it can form oval-shaped onions of enormous size, almost as big as cantaloupes. Since we are not after winning prizes at the local farm show, we are content with onions that we begin to harvest when they are the size of a hen's egg, and continue throughout late summer when they have got-ten perhaps as big as a large apple. Their only use is for eating fresh, in salads or sandwiches or sliced as a side dish to a grilled steak with potato. They seem the preeminent hamburger onion, sweet and mild, with none of the acridness that makes raw onions indigestible to many. They are not much good for cooking, being too watery and delicate of flavor, and their keeping qualities are nil. Even toward the end of summer, onions still left standing in the row will begin to show decayed centers of pale brown slime. So we enjoy them while we have them. Who, after all, expects fresh peas or green beans or cucumbers at all seasons?

For keeping qualities, we grow only one variety, the fascinating cippolini from Italy. One thinks of onions as perfect globes, or perhaps as rounded oval shapes. Cippolini are a curiosity, then, for they are round but flattened in the shape an imaginative child might draw an extraterrestrial spaceship. They range in size, even within the same row, from diminutive ones perfect for boiling and dressing with cream sauce for the Thanksgiving table, to sturdier ones as wide across as one's palm.

For those, we have a special use. We peel them carefully to preserve their shape. Then, we set each one on a square of baking parchment large enough to fold up around its sides and twist into a swirl at the top, mimicking its original skin. Before folding up the parchment, we put a square of butter, perhaps a tablespoon, on top, with a sprinkling of salt and fresh-ground pepper. If, when the parchment is drawn up around the onion and twirled, there is too much left over, we cut it away with scissors. We then put each separate onion package on a baking sheet with extra crumpled parchment beneath, so that the bottoms of the onions will not come into direct contact with the hot pan and burn. We bake the onions at 350° until a thin skewer pierced into one meets with no resistance. Depending on the size of the onions, baking may take between 45 minutes and an hour, but sealed up as they are, they may be held at 200° for some time while we get other things ready. Of course, we bring them to the table in their "skins."

It is a given that any vegetable garden will always be bursting at its seams. Like greenhouses, vegetable gardens should be stretchable somehow, because there are always new vegetables, and new varieties of old ones, and there are the old ones themselves. Who is going to give up growing Black-Seeded Simpson lettuce, no matter how many tempting new and heirloom varieties the seed catalogs offer us? So we have had to learn to make use of every inch of our vegetable garden space, by intercropping and succession sowing and by coming to learn which vegetables can stand crowding and which must absolutely stand open to the full sun. Onions belong to the latter class, and it is no good trying to plant them in rows between lettuces harvested in early summer, or even radishes.

So we will keep growing them, despite the sour words of two of our best vegetable garden mentors. For without onions, we would have less to draw from in spring and summer, no wonderful autumn harvest, and less satisfaction from our winter-baked onions patiently wrapped in parchment. If it were a store-bought onion, even a cippolino, one might still say, "Why bother?"

PIGS

One of the peculiarities of the English language is that we call the living one thing and the dead another—at least when it comes to the table. We hunt deer; we eat venison. We raise calves; we eat veal. We keep cattle; we eat sirloin. So it is with pigs, which are pigs only so long as they are alive but are transmogrified into pork, bacon, lard, and so on when dead.

We have both always eaten pork—with relish. Pork loin at Sunday dinner, pork chops when our mothers were feeling harried and had to produce a meal in a hurry, barbecue ribs on the Fourth of July. And for the last forty-one years we have kept pigs. The first was a little piglet a friend gave us while we still lived on Beacon Street in Boston a week before our scheduled move to a country farm. That piglet spent his first week with us in the bathtub. Showering with a pig is not a common experience.

Our first pig was named Morose not because of any sullen temperament, though she was certainly piglike and went about her essential business with extraordinary concentration. She had droopy eyelids and seemed to look on the world at large with a certain wise sadness.

That was the case when she contemplated her abundant dinner of mashed potatoes, cooked squash, and whole milk. Nourishing fare it was, generally, both for a pig and for the young people one of us spent our days caring for. They, not the pig, all attended the Fernald School, where children with special needs were enrolled by parents who could not, for various reasons, cope with the difficulties they had brought into the world. Some— always the most dear—were Down syndrome children, possessed of an unusual sweetness and a desire to cooperate. Others were autistic, locked in their own compulsions that were so difficult to understand from the outside, and sometimes so painful to observe, since some would hit themselves, hard, until retinas became detached and measurable brain damage occurred. Morose was a relief from all that, and she ate the bland food they left over each day in such quantity. Morose provided them with some amusement when we visited, for "outings" at the Fernald School were encouraged.

And generally, shocking as it may be to say so, her life was not much different from theirs, but in one regard. Morose was destined for the table.

We have not always named our pigs, though we did for many years. Morose was followed by Jane and Theresa (respectively) for one of our aunts and mothers, each of whom offset the cost of her upkeep with a generous portion of pork. After a year in Denmark, we named one pig Gorm the Old, after Denmark's first king. But the last pig we named came to an end so sad we abandoned the habit of naming or, more accurately, left it in the hands of those who largely tended them, preferring ourselves not to know which was which. Our last named pig was

Rolo for an image on a shopping bag of a happy big-eared boy with a wisp of curly hair sticking up on his head, which frankly looked so much like a caricature of our son to avoid the joke. But this story ends badly, if instructively. Rolo seemed a happy pig, certainly each morning and evening when we visited him with food and water. But in November, some weeks before we thought to slaughter him, he fell ill. The vet was summoned, and after much probing and study of his stool and urine, determined that Rolo had ulcers, probably bleeding. And though medicine was prescribed, Rolo grew sicker and died. Of course we asked the vet how he could have gotten ulcers and were abashed at his answer. Loneliness, he thought, simply too many hours spent waiting for our two brief visits each day. Pigs are social animals and they need company; humans will do, if not other pigs. But they must not be left in solitude. We have since then always kept two pigs even though we could never consume in a year the quantities of pork two pigs render. It pleases us that they have happy communal lives and we have fine pork to give our friends.

Over the years we have kept more than a few of the over one hundred breeds available, some endangered. Morose was a Yorkshire, often kept by commercial breeders because they produce large litters, and in fact she came from a commercial farm in Peabody, Massachusetts. Theresa and Jane were Landrace, bought from a local farmer. They were charming, with large floppy ears, and very vigorous, gaining weight quickly and yielding more pork in six months than any other breed we have kept. We saw many pigs during our year in Denmark, for many of our friends lived in the country and keeping pigs is very common there. So we came to know many breeds, and when we returned to America we sought out some that we had admired in Europe. Among the most beautiful were actually an old American breed, Hampshires, which, like Belted Galloway cows, are black with a pronounced white stripe encircling the forefront of the body. But two breeds caught our hearts both for beauty and productivity—Old

Spots and Tamworths. Old Spots are perhaps the most charming, with enormous floppy ears that almost cover the whole face. They are an English breed dating to the early nineteenth century and valued for their preferred diet, vegetables and apples, which we have in abundance for months in the late summer and fall, and for the rich fat they carry, which produces quantities of lard.

Tamworths are also an English breed and, like Old Spots, critically endangered. Their coats protect them from sunburn and they are great foragers, able to be let loose in our woods to find and consume quantities of beech mast. They are unusually long pigs, lean and largely free of excess fat. Though not good lard pigs, they are excellent for bacon, and so we try to keep both a Tamworth and an Old Spot each year.

Friends sometimes query us about slaughtering endangered breeds like Old Spots and Tamworths. But the very survival of these ancient breeds depends on their being consumed, for none will be preserved simply for sentimentality. They must continue to offer the table and the stockyard the qualities that made them cherished from the first: docility, ingenuity, beauty, and fine quality for the table. It is for just these reasons that the British royal family keeps them and joins with us in their preservation.

There is no farm animal more completely useful than a pig. Pigs are easy to raise, quick to put on weight, and every part of them is of use. And so for many centuries, that day in autumn when the pig is slaughtered is celebrated by the whole village as one of great importance. In Europe the customary method of slaughter is to bleed out the pig so that even the blood can be turned to something edible and delicious, in this case boudin noir or blood sausage. This sausage, though it usually contains other ingredients—pork, lard, spices—depends for its essential character on fresh pig blood and a lot of it, usually as much as a half gallon. And though we both enjoy eating it, we have never been able to endure watching the process.

We slaughter our pigs in quite a different and, we hope, a more humane fashion. We have for many years had the services of Bob Gulley, a neighbor and a longtime Vermont farmer well versed in the old traditions. He is also, having lived his whole life in intimate relation to them, extraordinarily good with animals. They feel at ease with him, and in the process of slaughtering anything it is essential that the animal experience no fear or foreboding. For that would be both inhumane and harmful to the meat because of the hormones associated with fear.

On the morning, usually in late October, when we slaughter the pigs, their pen is freshly swept and dressed with new hay. They are then separated, one taken to the back pasture, the other left inside. Bob's pockets are always filled with apples, and so he sits in the fresh hay and pulls them from his pocket one by one to the delight of the fated pig. And then he shoots it in the head, causing almost instant death. Only then is the blood bled out and, at least by us, never collected. The pig is carried down to the scalding kettle, the pen cleaned, the pastured pig brought back, and the whole process played out again. And then the worst is done, for it is true that even those of us who are confirmed carnivores find that moment between life and death unsettling.

The rest occurs by time-honored ritual. The whole pig is immersed in a vast cauldron of boiling water and then scraped clean of all its bristly coat. The innards are removed, some saved, certainly the liver, kidneys, and heart, and some, by us at least, disposed of, though no self-respecting French or Italian farmer tosses the intestines into the burial pit.

There is about this day always an aura of both solemnity and joy. We take the life of a sentient being, one we have come to know and whom we hope we have treated with kindness, and by that act we feed ourselves for the ensuing year. Joyful and solemn in equal measure—almost a synecdoche for the whole experience of a country life.

Chicharrones
(Crispy Pork Belly)

1 pound pork belly, cut into cubes
2 cups water
1 tablespoon sea salt
Fresh-ground pepper
Lime wedges

Place the pork, skin side down, in one layer in a pan. Add water and salt. Bring to a boil over high heat and cook until all the water evaporates.

Once the water is gone, lower the heat and let the pork get crispy and golden in its own fat.

Serve with a dust of pepper and lime wedges.

SERVES 4
From the kitchen of Beatrice Tosti di Valminuta

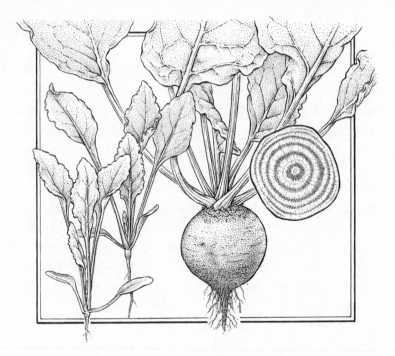

BEETS

During the years we taught school, Christmas vacation seemed the almost perfect time to take a trip. Neither of our families was of the sort to require our presence for the holidays, and the few times we did venture home we felt vaguely in the way, unless, indeed, we did the cooking, which was not our idea of a vacation. We used that precious period of freedom usually to go to San Francisco, and later, to Europe. The habit of sidestepping Christmas has persisted since, almost always as a trip to Europe, where good meals are almost equal in pleasure to painting or architecture. But we are not completely without holiday spirit, and so the choice of a restaurant for Christmas Day is among the most crucial we make. With only a little effort, we can remember most of them. A few spring immediately to mind, such as the foie gras feast we had in Paris, the richness of the various dishes interrupted by three tiny sweetened sorbets made separately of carrots, beets, and turnips.

Beets figured again in a remarkable restaurant we ate in on Christmas Day in Amsterdam called De Silveren Spiegel (the Silver Mirror). It is one of the oldest in the city, located in two beautiful dark old town houses built in 1614. Immaculate white tables were set among its blackened walls and beams, and there were indeed many old mirrors, their imperfect, rippled surfaces tossing candlelight back and forth. We went through a huge number of courses, of fish and little game birds and rich, deep stews, but what we remember best were the beets, which had been rubbed in butter, then wrapped tightly in parchment and baked very slowly for many hours. Stripped of their skins, the results were almost like candy, a counterpoint to the slightly bitter ragout with which they were served.

Beets figure rarely on the menus of American restaurants, and most Americans would quickly confess that they are not among their favorite vegetables. Perhaps there are too many childhood memories of not being allowed to leave the table until that ill-cooked pile of dark purple was consumed, or worse, taken sour-pickled straight from the jar. Beets were supposed to be good for you, but we knew one child who bluntly opined, "I don't *like* anything that is good for me!" This relative lack of enthusiasm among Americans is curious, because beets are among the most popular vegetables in Germany, Central Europe, and Russia, as in the famous borscht, which Americans of non-Russian descent mostly enjoy as "an acquired taste."

It may be that many American cooks simply do not have time for beets, since ideally sized ones at two to three inches in circumference take thirty to forty minutes of boiling, and larger ones may require as much as two hours. If they are baked in the manner most good cooks prefer—and as the Silver Mirror served them—then they require as long as five hours in a very slow oven. The cooking process itself is also messy, since beets are always cooked with their roots, skins, and two inches of their tops left on, lest they bleed excessively and lose color and flavor. They are judged done when a fork or skewer pierces them with only slight resistance. Then each beet must be taken in hand and its skin slipped off. A hot beet is no more pleasant than the proverbially dropped hot potato, but if they have been boiled, they can be deskinned under cool running water and then returned to the liquid in which they were cooked for a gentle reheating. If you bake them, you simply have to take courage in hand and work fast, or perhaps have heatproof mittens. Either way, a bit of butter gives the beets a lovely shine.

Like most vegetables cultivated since prehistoric times, beets share a long and fascinating history with humanity. The original beet is a native of the Canary Islands and Madeira to the Atlantic coast of Europe, across the Mediterranean, and well into southern Russia, Syria, and Iraq. Such geographic diversity partially explains why beets have been so climatically adaptable. Originally they grew near water, in fact just above the high-tide line, and were gathered as greens. The Romans ate the roots, but they knew them as long carrotlike structures, and in fact, occasionally a beet in a garden row reverts to that original form.

Beets came to America with the first colonists and were crucial to their diet well into the late nineteenth century. That was because they were adapted to a wide variety of climates and soils, could be sown as early in spring as the soil could be worked, and resown two or three times for winter storage crops. Barrels of them were put down in sand and kept in a cool place to be extracted all winter long. They were a primary food in getting past "the Six Weeks of Want" (sometimes called "the Hungry Gap"), a period roughly from the end of January to the middle of March, when supplies of most stored vegetables would have been exhausted. By early March, beets left in storage would begin to sprout, providing much treasured green food, the first seen since late autumn. Then, as beets are biennials, the remaining roots would be planted out to garner seed for the following spring's sowing. It was a thriftless household that ate up all its stored beets, though sometimes necessity compelled that. Fortunately, we can now depend on seed houses, though devoted seed savers still store and replant beets to maintain historic heirloom varieties. We should all be grateful to them for their trouble, since they sustain a rich gene pool, stretching back perhaps two thousand years, on which we may all have to depend if the highly selected forms often offered us ever fail.

However, most of us shake out the contents of a packet into the palm of our hand, caper-sized seeds with a few sharp points. Actually, each seed is several seeds in a dry husk, a sort of fruit, rather like an orange. And from each seed will come two, three, or four individual seedlings. We sow our beets in rather short rows, perhaps eight feet long and two feet apart in furrows one inch deep. We space them about an inch apart, with the expectation that we will have to thin them radically, and perhaps twice, so that the plants will eventually stand approximately four inches apart. (If you are lazy about the thinning, the beets will be too small to use, except perhaps for one that found a little extra space at the end or to the side of a row.)

Thinning is itself a minor art of vegetable gardening, requiring that you be either extremely limber or kneel upon the ground between the rows. So as not to disturb the seedling you mean to keep, slip your index and third finger around the one to be eliminated in a sort of scissor effect, pressing against the earth and extracting the seedling gently between your fingers with your other hand. Ideally, you try to keep the strongest seedlings, but occasionally the spacing is wrong, and you will have to extract a strong one and leave a weaker one. In that case, it is good to know that beets are among the few root crops that may be transplanted. Keep a bowl of mud and water near you, rather like a too-loose mud pie, and place each seedling into it. When ready to transplant, extract each seedling carefully (you may want to add more water) and replant it into a prepared row, taking care that its crown is exactly at the level it originally grew.

In our experience, beets have few troubles, the worst perhaps being our acidic soil, which causes the same sort of scabs and lesions it can on potatoes. The remedy is a liberal dusting of lime, preferably in autumn but at the latest in early spring, two or so weeks before the beet seed is sown. Rotation is also important, though fortunately, beets can tolerate half a day of shade and still produce acceptable crops, a boon in smaller gardens with one shady end. Occasionally, beet tops look stunted and a pinched, dark green, indicating the need for phosphorus, which can be applied as a balanced granular fertilizer or by an organic alternative. Improvement is almost immediate.

The preferred table beet should grow small rounded roots that quickly reach a circumference of two to three inches with small leaves, though if you like beet greens, there are beets grown specifically for that purpose (not including chard), and carrot-rooted forms have been preserved. Much like the cabbage early in its cultivated history, beets were bred for highly specialized uses, so that table beets, chard, mangel-wurzels, and sugar beets are in fact all *Beta vulgaris*, one botanical entity with formative but not botanical differences. Table beets are botanically grouped under *Beta vulgaris* var. *crassa* (meaning thick or fleshy), and within the group are hundreds of choices, some of great antiquity, and many designed for specific purposes. Bull's Blood, for example, produces the deepest Burgundy-red foliage we know, and though its roots are not among the most flavorful, we always put some young leaves into an early summer salad, where their black-purple color is beautiful among various clear shades of lettuce and arugula and such. Most gardeners have their own favorites, and seed companies are helpful in indicating early, midseason, and storage beets. Chioggia is a favorite here, for its beautiful concentric circles of red rose, waxy yellow, and white, sometimes with the colors bled over one another. It is always important, too, to grow a good, strong beet of an appropriate color especially for storage. We have tried many (and will try more), but standards are Red Ace and Merlin. For those to whom childhood experiences with beets bring back too many unpleasant memories, there are "golden beets," which we find insipid, or pure white ones, best perhaps eaten raw.

At harvesttime, as late in the year as we can still stand to work in sleet and snow, we dig any beet we have not eaten and put them all down in barely moist sand in the old way, though not in whiskey barrels but in the huge old terra-cotta pots we use about the garden for summer-blooming annuals. Under the conditions of the shop adjoining the lower greenhouse, shuttered against the light with temperatures that hover around 40 degrees, they keep sound throughout the winter and into early spring.

We have already indicated our favorite cooking method for beets, which is the slow bake in parchment. You can use aluminum foil, but you will lose some of the glamour offered by the Silver Mirror in Amsterdam. Four or five hours of cooking anything takes some planning, of course, and so perhaps it is part of Saturday or Sunday's supper. Always cook more than you think you need, for the beets may shrink by as much as half. Once the beets are in the oven at about 250°, you should have something else to do. They require little attention, and after they are cooked, they can sit in a barely warm oven until they need to be reheated, peeled, buttered, and served.

Cooking has so many values—feeding good things both to oneself and to others, showing care for the texture of one's life—and it is always both a learning experience and an artistic expression, for even a recipe you know well and have prepared a thousand times can still teach you some way to do it better. Another value of preparing a meal, seldom commented on, is that it can contain the memory of a particularly happy experience and thus be a postcard one sent to oneself long ago and only just rediscovered.

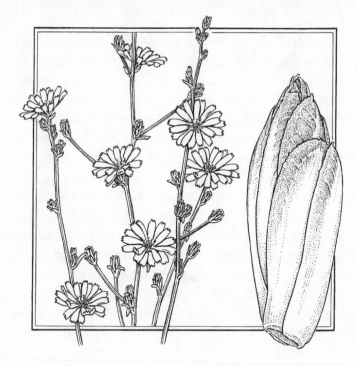

BELGIAN ENDIVE

In August and September in New England and in other parts of
North America, the roadsides are made glorious by the flowers
of wild chicory, *Chicorium intybus* var. *sativum*. Like many wildflowers, it cannot compete with the vigorous pasture grasses
grown for hay. But it flourishes in thin soils beside country roads,
made even poorer by the sand and salt spread over roads to melt
winter snow and ice. Its companions are likely to be simple field
daisies, progenitors, after many crosses and backcrosses, of the
Shasta daisy of gardens and Queen Anne's lace, the ancestor of
all carrots. They are all "wildflowers," and where mowing is
done along road verges only once in late June, they form thick
carpets of flower, gardens in themselves, for miles and miles.

But none of them are truly wildflowers in the sense of being
natives, and least of all the wild chicory, which came into America

not by accident—in fodder or hay seeds as the other two did—but as a cultivated crop. All the plants one sees, with their limpid blue daisies opening on bright late-summer mornings and closing at noon, are descendants of seed brought by the early colonists as garden plants, and in parts of North America they are still called by their colonial name, succory. Grown not for their leaves but for their long carrotlike roots, they were make-do plants that, when parched and ground, were a substitute for coffee. Later, when coffee became more plentiful but still a luxury, they were used as an additive, a practice still followed in Louisiana, where coffee without chicory is just not coffee. For all its beauty along late-summer roadsides, *Chicorium intybus* var. *sativum* has little value in modern gardens, except possibly as a flower, where its clear blue two-inch-wide daisies can be heartbreakingly beautiful grown with a late sowing of scarlet field poppies, *Papaver rhoeas*. One could call that effect almost the soul of late summer.

Roadside chicory has many relatives within the genus *Chicorium*, and for centuries they have been enormously useful as garden greens. *Chicorium* is a Latinized version of an ancient Arabic word, and it is one of those genuses of ancient lineage, like cabbage, which, through thousands of years of selection, have branched into a number of forms that most gardeners would assume to be separate species. But they are all genetically descended from one wild progenitor, so whether one is growing escarole or endive, chicon frisée, radicchio, or puntarelle, they are all chicories and they will all freely intercross. Since many are winter hardy, as is the roadside chicory, they are a nightmare for the home seed saver, who might, in one generation, end up with almost anything, for good or ill.

The fine autumn chicories we treasure so much for late salads, for sautéed bitter greens with garlic, and for grilling are all treated under our discussion of fall vegetables, such as beets, carrots, celeriac, etc. But one chicory is an invaluable winter green. It is Belgian endive, so-called not because the plant originates in

Belgium, but because it can be forced to perfection in caves there that maintain a constant temperature of around 40 degrees in winter. For that reason it is often also called by its Flemish name, Whitloof, which means "white leaf," since the forcing process is done in darkness and leaves little chlorophyll (and less bitterness) in the leaves.

There are actually a few shallow caves in Vermont, but none, as it happens, are on our property. We could perhaps dig one on our hillside, for old settlers around here did, and we know of two that survive in the neighboring town of Whitingham. However, we already have a facility where we can force winter endives from Thanksgiving until well into April. It is the shop, attached to the lower greenhouse, where we store all our winter vegetables. Its casement windows are thrown wide open in summer to provide an airy dining space for more guests than we can seat at our kitchen table, and it then becomes a dining room buried deep in the garden. But in winter its wooden shutters are closed tight against the cold, and it then becomes a rather gloomy space, dank and chilly but just above freezing, not unlike—in our imagination, at least—the caves of Belgium.

Growing endives in our climate is very easy, for they relish a long, cool season, and that is pretty much the definition of Vermont in summer. Ideally, seed should be sown just when the ground is workable in early spring, but usually broad beans and peas and spinach and the early lettuces have priority, so the forcing chicory is sown somewhere around the early part of April. As we do not aim for vast winter chicories the thickness of a man's wrist, that is soon enough. The seed is sown in a drill about a half inch deep, in rich, well-composted soil, and covered lightly with earth. If we can, we sow seed about a half inch apart, though some thinning is always required, using the two-fingered scissor method, in which the index and third finger are pressed close around the plant to be removed, and the finger and thumb of the other hand pluck the unwanted seedling out. Since Belgian endive is raspy, it does not serve, as other thinned spring greens do, for tossing into a mixed salad. But the thinnings make the chickens and the geese very happy, so they are not wasted.

Like most leafy vegetables, all chicories do a creditable job of their main purpose in life—or in our life—in half a day of sun. So they are ideal candidates, along with lettuces, celery, and celeriac, for the shadier part of the garden, which all of us seem to have. But wherever they are sown, they need to occupy that row for a full growing season, from midspring to autumn. Dig and sort them after the first mild frosts have come to force them into dormancy. Then cut away the tops an inch above the growing crown, and pack them away for forcing. The succulent shoots will begin to appear in late November and can be harvested throughout the winter. If you take care not to sever the Whitloof too close to the living crown, there is even a second harvest, not of neatly formed loaves but of loose, pale gold "greens," a welcome relief when dinner salads have become largely composed of shredded cabbage. And there is even a third harvest possible, for the pale, spent roots can be planted in the garden or along the roadside for pretty flowers later in the summer. They will probably be of a paler blue than the roadside chicories, or even a faded mauve, but they are still quite pretty.

We used to store our chicory roots in damp sand, as we do our beets and carrots and celeriac. But like winter leeks, chicories are leaves, and it is nice to serve them sliced or quartered. Sand gets in the way, for wash them how you will, there is always that unpleasant abrasion of grit against the teeth. So now we store them in barely damp peat, each root stood close to its neighbor, with only a little space between. It is pleasant, on a cold winter day, to slip one's fingers into the cool moist peat, feeling for a fat chicory, and severing it neatly for the winter harvest basket.

The American seed company Johnny's Selected Seeds has recently marketed a Belgian endive that does not need all this bother of potting up in moist sand or peat. It is a Dutch variety called Totem, which needs only to be stored in a moist, cool place and then taken out and stood upright to form a tight bullet-shaped head. In theory, you could simply employ an old used refrigerator in the garage to cool the roots. We are tempted by Totem, for the picture in the catalog is very attractive. We would still pack our roots in moist peat, however, in the same way that we always plant our paperwhite narcissus in real compost, and root them in the bulb closet before bringing them on to bloom. We are perhaps silly for thinking that a paperwhite narcissus or a simple chicory root dug from the garden in autumn and asked to grow again in a dark, cool room has a life of its own. But we would never just line up the chicory roots in a paper box and wait for the results. Or plant the paperwhite bulbs in gravel and water. It seems unfair to them, somehow.

Once we were in a supermarket, where we heard a harried young woman say, half to herself and half to us, "Why can't they create another kind of meat!" One of us replied, "Well, there's guinea fowl." That was a mistake, as it happened, like most spon-taneous comments in supermarkets or dentists' offices are a mis-take. She turned away from us as if we had made a racial slur. But a plump young guinea fowl—if you can get one—is wonderful, braised with a liberal handful of fresh herbs and some wine. An old one may taste like a stewed football—we know, for we have tried—but the broth is ambrosial. Still, guinea is one thing you might cook when you have gone through beef, pork, chicken, and lamb.

And in the same vein, if you have committed to living sea-sonally, as we have, and you begin to weary of all the things you have put by in cold sand—when you have gone through the beets, carrots, and celeriac—and the potatoes dry-stored—when the Brussels sprouts on the stalks have all been snapped off and you begin to fear beriberi or scurvy or whatever bad things used to happen to transatlantic sailors when they began to crave something crunchy and green, forced Belgian endive is the answer. In winter, it is a great comfort.

Most commonly, Belgian endive is eaten raw, the leaves detached and tossed with blander lettuce leaves for a pleasant bitter taste. But they may also be sliced or quartered, drizzled with olive oil and vinegar, and eaten alone. (Rice wine vinegar, because of its sweetness, cuts nicely against the bitter taste.) Lately, also, they are served as canapés, the single, boat-shaped leaves filled with savory chopped ingredients. Unless the filling is very savory indeed, a well-seasoned meat or fish salad, for example, it may be the convenience of the leaves as finger food at cocktail parties that mostly recommends them.

But one of the most interesting ways to serve Belgian endive is as a braised vegetable. Leave them whole and place them in one layer in an ovenproof baking dish, covered halfway up with rich chicken stock and dotted over their tops with butter and fresh-ground pepper. Place the baking dish on top of the stove and bring the liquid to a simmer until it is reduced by about half. Put a sheet of buttered baking parchment or waxed paper cut to the size of the baking dish on top, and slip the dish into a slow oven—about 325°—until the liquid is absorbed and the endive is quite tender and a lovely golden brown, about half an hour. The results are the vegetable equivalent of the guinea fowl. And the dish would be very good served with one.

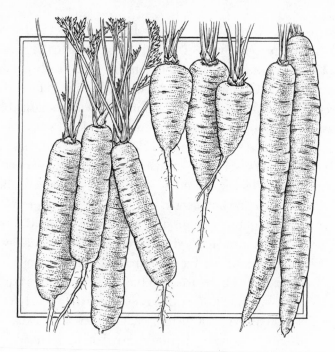

CARROTS

Queen Anne's lace, though it is among the most loved of American wildflowers, is native not to America but rather to Europe and Southwest Asia. And in fact, specimens that grace fields and roadsides throughout our country may well be early escapees of forms of the domestic garden carrot grown in colonial gardens. Henri Vilmorin, the great early nineteenth-century French seedsman, found a particularly thick-rooted specimen of Queen Anne's lace growing on the Belgian coast, and within four generations marketed it in 1839 as White Belgian. It is still available, and many consider it among the most fragrant of all carrots. Nori Pope, who with his wife, Sandra, created beautiful borders at Hadspen House, also told us that the easiest way to have the flowers of Queen Anne's lace in the perennial border was to buy tired old carrots from the supermarket in early spring—those already showing hairy white roots and probably put on the bargain rack—and simply plant them with their tops even to the ground.

That piece of information interested us particularly not only because we love Queen Anne's lace but also because in forty years of vegetable gardening our only failure with carrots came from transplanting. Highly skilled gardeners can do it, when plants are quite tiny, and the invention of flexible plastic cell packs has now made the transplanting of many sensitive plants—poppies, for example, or morning glories—possible as it has never been before. Slip each one out, gently, like ice cubes from a tray. But transplanted from the open ground, carrots are generally intractable, and the transplanter who caused our failure was by no means a skilled gardener but an impatient child sent out for a handful of parsley. He returned to the kitchen with the parsley and this announcement: "I tried to get some carrots, too, but they were all too small, so I put them back." Not one survived.

Apparently, however, a mature carrot that has spent a winter in cold storage can be replanted and will successfully sprout and produce flowers, perhaps a tiny bit dingier than Queen Anne's lace but still beautiful in form, with dainty, lacy umbels borne to a height of three feet above ferny leaves. This is the method seed savers in cold climates employ, and it has resulted in the preservation of many antique, heirloom, and novelty varieties.

For us at least, carrots are very easy to grow, provided we can offer them the sunniest part of the vegetable garden and the steady moisture they require. Our soils are deep and rich, made so after more than twenty years of cultivation and the addition of copious amounts of rotted manure and compost. That is the sort of thing a carrot likes best, though it is prepared to compromise, provided its questing roots meet up with no stones. The shallower your soil, the squatter the carrot you choose to grow should be, though there is nothing quite like extracting a foot-and-a-half-long carrot from the earth in autumn.

Eight inches of good tilth should allow most carrots to

expand to a length of six or so inches, and modern varieties have been bred to be fatter and more cylindrical than tapered and long. In some soils, germination can be a problem, especially heavy clay after a rainfall, for carrot seed, which is tiny, has trouble breaking through the crust of what old gardeners called "a panned soil." One solution is to sow the seed in a half-inch furrow and then fill it with perlite or vermiculite; another, practiced in nineteenth-century gardens, was to sow radishes with the carrots, for they are sturdy little things, able to shoulder away the soil for their frailer companions. Whatever method is used, the sprouted seed will have to be thinned, though unless you are aiming to win a prize at the country fair, carrots can be grown closer together than most other root vegetables, as close as two inches one from another. To thin seedlings, use the scissors method described in "Beets." But do not attempt transplanting extra seedlings; simply sow more seed, perhaps of another variety.

"Variety" is the word for carrots, since there is hardly another vegetable that comes in so many shapes and colors, from spherical balls the size of plums to great pointed roots two feet in length. Colors can vary from the familiar carrot color through deeper orange, yellow, red, purple, near black, and white. Indeed, some seed houses offer a rainbow mix, which will give you all the colors from one row. Uncarroty-colored carrots, such as the deep purple varieties Purple Haze and Deep Purple, are stunning in a carrot salad, though we have not found them to have the finest flavor.

The extraordinary number of carrot varieties, which seems to increase with every spring catalog, is in part the result of an unusual genetic diversity. The carrot of our gardens combines genetic material from worlds as far apart as northern Europe and Afghanistan, with more than two thousand years of breeding and interbreeding. Carrots almost appear to be the white rats, or the fruit flies, of vegetable gardening, for it seems that you can breed them to be anything. But in addition to providing fascinating novelties, this proliferation has its point. For shape in a carrot matters according to the earth it must grow in. Deep, richly tilled soil produces long straight carrots, but stony soil causes them to twist, and shallow soils stunt them. Complexity of flavor varies as well, from richly carroty to woody and uninteresting, however splendid the color might be. The flavors and fragrances of carrots would be enough to test the powers of the most descriptively gifted wine scholar. Indeed, one could have a *dégustation de carottes*, if one grew enough varieties and could stand to spit them out.

Finally, it is texture that matters most in a carrot. Some, like the redoubtable Nantes, are good eaten raw or in salads, and are amazingly crunchy and sweet when dug fresh from the ground. But they are no good at all in a carrot cake, for example, or a French braise, because for those one wants a firmer, dryer carrot such as Danvers or Chantenay. So the home gardener must choose carrot varieties for both fresh eating in summer and winter storage. Neither should be neglected, for they are distinct pleasures, both carrotlike but otherwise quite different.

If we were forced to choose, perhaps we would fall to the side of garden-fresh carrots, which never need peeling and have a crunch no supermarket carrot can equal. They can be eaten out of hand or cut into a carrot salad, a guilelessly simple dish made of fresh carrots, julienned, a small onion cut in half and then into slices as thin as you can make them, dressed lightly with good olive oil and balsamic vinegar, salt and pepper, and perhaps a pinch of dried oregano. Lately, we have been adding a scant half teaspoon of hot red pepper paste imported from Calabria, the sharp pungent taste of which serves as counterpoint to the sweetness of the carrots.

But if we grew carrots only for eating fresh, we would miss the pleasure of trekking through the snow on a cold winter day, entering the lower greenhouse and passing through its warm lushness, sweet with the smell of fragrant cyclamen and a single large *Edgeworthia*, and then into the darkened earth-smelling shop to dig three or four winter carrots from the sand they are stored in, buried deep in huge old terra-cotta pots. Our winter soups, stews, and braises would suffer, too, at least in our minds, because though we *could* use store-bought carrots, and the organically grown ones are often very good, it just wouldn't feel the same.

Nor would our carrot cake. In this book we offer few recipes written in the usual form, with a cup of this and a teaspoon of that. But cakes are exacting in their measurement of ingredients, and so here is our recipe.

Carrot Cake

1½ cups sugar
1¼ cups vegetable oil
4 eggs
2 cups flour
2 teaspoons baking powder
¼ teaspoon baking soda
1 teaspoon salt
2 teaspoons cinnamon
½ teaspoon ground cloves
½ teaspoon allspice
1 cup yellow raisins
1 cup coarsely broken pecans
1 teaspoon vanilla extract
Enough peeled and coarsely grated carrots to make
    3 cups

Preheat the oven to 325°. Butter and flour two 8-inch cake pans and set aside.

In a large bowl, combine the sugar, oil, and eggs, and beat until smooth.

Sift together all the dry ingredients into another bowl. Add the raisins and nuts and toss them until they are coated. Add the raisin mixture to the sugar mixture, beating well. Add the vanilla and carrots, and combine thoroughly.

Divide the mixture evenly into the two pans, thump them to level the batter, and bake until a toothpick inserted in the center comes out clean, about 25–30 minutes.

Remove the cakes from the pans and cool on racks. Ice with cream cheese icing.

Cream Cheese Icing

1 package (8 ounces) Philadelphia cream cheese, at
    room temperature
½ cup (1 stick) salted butter, at room temperature
1 box (16 ounces) powdered sugar

In a large bowl, mix the cream cheese and butter and beat until light and fluffy. Add the powdered sugar and beat until smooth.

Pasta with Carrots and Zucchini

Sea salt (coarse and fine)
1 pound big rigatoni
5 carrots, sliced
3 zucchini (not too big), sliced the same way
2 onions, sliced
2 fistfuls of fresh basil
½ cup extra-virgin olive oil
Ground black pepper
Grated Parmesan cheese

Bring water to a roaring boil in a large pot. Add the salt and pasta. Stir and cover the pot to bring the water back to a boil as fast as possible. Once it boils, uncover and stir. Lower the flame and place the lid over half the pot, stirring every minute or so.

As soon as you start the water, place the rest of the ingredients except the cheese (using only ¾ of the basil) and some salt in a large skillet over high heat. As soon as the vegetables start to catch color, lower the flame to medium-high and cook until the liquid is reduced and the vegetables are nice and caramelized.

Taste for seasoning. Add pasta *very* al dente and the remaining basil and stir so the pasta absorbs the sauce. Add some pasta water to tie together all the flavors. Sprinkle with the cheese.

SERVES 4

From the kitchen of Beatrice Tosti di Valminuta

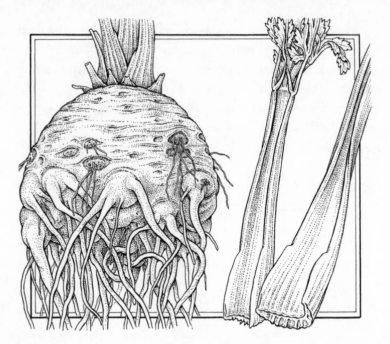

CELERIAC

Our little house is rich in small treasures we have brought home from trips away—from Baja, California, a large terra-cotta bowl we use for oil-baked tomatoes; a Georgian silver stuffing spoon bought at the Portobello Road in London one Christmas forty years ago; a basket from Botswana so tightly woven that it holds water, bought at the crafts show that was held for many years on San Francisco's Fort Mason Pier. Clothes, too, some of which will last a lifetime, such as a large collection of jacquard Achile socks that we found first in New York, and then at Samaritaine in Paris, and lately at Citizen, a tiny men's shop in the Castro in San Francisco. We have brought plants also, from every place we could, packed into boxes and shipped in the hold, or, if they were very tender, delivered to the flight attendant as an imposition on first-class storage, for we always travel coach. If we could not bring plants, we brought seeds, especially from Vilmorin in Paris and Franchi Sementi in Rome. In this way, we have deepened and enriched life in our house in southern Vermont, which has come over the years almost to contain the world for us.

Many of the things we have brought home are for the table, which has always been deeply at the center of our life here. So there is porcelain from Denmark, hand-painted by two old ladies and patiently accumulated during the year we lived there, because they painted only a piece a week. There is silver from the silver vaults in London that are deep underground. A large, heavy faience fish plate from Rome, circular and green-painted, sits on the dining table and is always full of seasonal fruit. And there are pots and pans, hundred-year-old copper and iron, that hang from our kitchen ceiling beams and are in constant use.

But it is not only solid treasures of metal, porcelain, or glass that we have brought home. For sheer weight and mass—and perhaps to many, for sheer improbability—nothing equaled our yearly suitcase of celery root. At the end of our annual winter stay in San Francisco, the evening before our flight, we would walk to the Cala Market at the corner of Hyde and California Streets, empty suitcase in hand, and bid a longing farewell to the heaps of freshly harvested artichokes, the beautiful lettuces in variety, the crunchy orange persimmons, none of which were available in markets near us. We were tempted by all of them, but we had come for celeriac and would heap up as much as would fill our suitcase. For unlike all the other produce we coveted, celeriac would keep, and in the bottom of the refrigerator, carefully wrapped, would last us the whole rest of the winter. At that time, it was rare for anyone to bring their own containers to the supermarket, and so, as we packed, we got stares, and sometimes even a puzzled question. It was a very odd thing, in that time, to do anything that seemed odd, in San Francisco.

Neither of us had eaten celery root as children, and we wonder if any American did, except perhaps abroad. But we were both very fond of the crunchy white base of the celery stalk with its small, pale gold ribs. Our mothers would set them aside for us when they filled the larger ribs with cream cheese and sprinkled them with paprika, a preparation that was a postwar staple of every middle-class cocktail party. We first met celery root itself at a dinner party in the early 1970s, given by a colleague who taught with us during our year in Copenhagen. Cut into julienne and dressed with vinegar, oil, and a little mayonnaise, it looked rather liked uncooked French fries. But when we tried it, it tasted of the best part of those remembered celery hearts. When we returned to America, it was unavailable in even the most sophisticated Boston markets. But we found it in San Francisco. And so we began to tote.

Carrying a suitcase of celeriac back each winter from California was certainly as much effort as growing our own could ever be. Still, it was years before we harvested our first crop. Prior to that, we quite enjoyed our little ritual, since both of us generally like going to trouble, and besides, each celeriac remoulade reminded us of where we had been and returned us, a little, to that experience. More practically, celeriac must be seeded quite early in the year, at least by the end of February, and then grown in cool temperatures and good light till it can be set out in the garden in late May. Cool temperatures are very easy to manage in Vermont, but such good light as we had was already devoted to pots of forced bulbs and the tender plants we had accumulated. In our greenhouse there was simply no room for baby celeriacs.

Then a chance visit to Jack and Karen Manix's Walker Farm in Dummerston, Vermont, changed our garden practices in many ways. They have tended a farm continuously in Jack's family since the eighteenth century, and they are good growers of long experience, primarily, at that time, of vegetables. They were willing to handle all the seed we could accumulate in our travels, and so many a good thing came into our garden, and also into their farm stand. At that time, specialty and foreign import seed houses lay in the future; puntarelle, radicchio, soybeans, fennel, and celeriac were still either rare or unavailable. Now they are easy of access in specialty markets like Whole Foods. That is of course wonderful, though we at least feel that some of the fun has been taken out. And one pays a price.

Of all the new things we were able to grow with the help of the Manixes, celeriac proved the easiest. It is primarily a Northern European crop, requiring a long, cool growing season. It thrives best in very fertile, deep, rich soil, a thing we easily achieve here through the generosity of all our livestock. It also is unusual among vegetables in relishing very moist soils, and one corner of our vegetable garden is always permanently moist from a spring on the hillside above it. So we have had success with celeriac in our own garden for twenty years, and the suitcase, a cheap brown vinyl thing glorified only by the cargo it carried, has long since gone to the town dump.

From seedlings sown in midwinter, celeriac is set out in May, and it occupies its ground well into late September or even early October, so it is a permanent part of the summer vegetable garden. It is a handsome plant, recognizably celerylike, for it and celery are genetically identical, specialized selections of a single wild progenitor, *Apium graveolens*. But the leaves of celeriac flare from the enlarged root, and are thinner though a darker green. They emit a strong celery scent when crushed, tempting us to use a few in a summer soup or salad, though we have found them unpleasantly bitter. Leaves and stems are not the point, anyway, for it is the roots one wants, and they should be dug as late in the season as possible before frosts. Taken from the ground, they will be as large as a fist, or perhaps even larger. Trim away the leaves, leaving about an inch of stem above the top of the root, for if you cut into the root itself, it will die, turning into a nasty mush. Keeping qualities are actually improved by leaving on the dirt that clings to the root. We used to enclose each root in cling wrap or a plastic bag and store them in a heap in the bottom of the refrigerator. But we found the smell of earth (and the occasional earthworm that always managed to wiggle out) somehow unsettling up against cold pot roast for tomorrow's lunch sandwiches. So now they are all bundled into a plastic garbage bag and tucked into the coldest corner of the winter garden. There, they keep perfectly sound until the last one is eaten in early April.

When a celeriac is brought into the kitchen, it is not a pretty thing, especially when it is encrusted with living mud. But even from Whole Foods it is not beautiful, encased in a thick skin that is all knobs and protruding roots. All that must be peeled away, resulting in what seems a good bit of waste, but leaving a smooth, roundish white knob behind. At this point, and at every stage thereafter, the naked celeriac must be kept in water that has been acidulated with white vinegar, else it will turn brown. The classic preparation is a remoulade. It is a lovely winter salad in which the celeriac is cut into thin slices and then into matchsticks, submerged in boiling acidulated water only for two or three minutes, refreshed under cold water to crispen it, spun dry, and then lightly coated with a dressing of vinegar and oil. But celeriac is equally delicious cut into rough chunks and sautéed in butter until it is tender, to accompany a steak or a roast chicken. It is always good in vegetable soups, and some people puree it with butter or add it to mashed potatoes. We are not so fond of purees, as they seem to remind us of baby food, and we think—pure prejudice on our part—that mashed potatoes should taste like mashed potatoes . . . and garlic.

However, there is one use of celeriac to which we are absolutely bound by sentiment. The evening before Thanksgiving, dinner is always oyster stew, a very old American custom that reminds us that oysters were once common food, nothing special, and that whole barrels of them were consumed, much as we now eat hot dogs. Our oyster stew is rich with our own chicken broth, cubed potatoes and celeriac, parsley from the summer parsley pot, heavy cream, the oyster liquid and, at the last minute, the plump oysters themselves are added, barely allowed to curl in the hot soup. Tiny, thumbnail-sized crackers—usually called "common crackers" in Vermont and oyster crackers most everywhere else—are passed around to sprinkle over individual bowls, and this abstemious repast prepares us for the abundance of the following day.

Accumulating celeriacs was never our primary reason for going to San Francisco every winter, and now that we grow our own, it is even less so. Still, when we are there, and in the market, we feel a twinge when we pass the pile of celery roots, and we look at our basket, half expecting to see the old brown vinyl suitcase.

CITRUS

In *Joy of Cooking*, Irma Rombauer begins her recipe for No-Knead Light Rolls with this sentence: "These are the rolls we remember from childhood: light as a feather and served in a special soft linen napkin." Most of us remember that napkin, probably a lone survivor from a damask set of a dozen, made soft by many bleachings and washings, treasured just because it always was *the* roll basket napkin. But all households have special dishes or utensils that are used for only certain foods or at certain times. There is of course the Thanksgiving turkey platter, too big for general use but always washed off and put out for that holiday. Cut-glass bowls have been passed down for generations solely to contain cranberry relish. In Southern homes there is the corn bread plate, never used for anything else, and usually a worn wooden bowl for mixing and kneading buttermilk biscuits.

Here, there is an old French faience plate, thick clay, dull white and brushed at the edges with a grass-green glaze, dimpled to hold stuffed eggs. It could never be used for any other purpose.

And there is our lemon dish, which usually sits on the living room mantel with two other ancient pieces of Asian pottery but comes to the table whenever we harvest a fresh lemon or lime. It was a gift many years ago from a friend, and actually we know little about it except that it is very old, perhaps even archaeological. It consists of a fluted pedestal on which a shallow dish five inches across is mounted, and it seems to have a greater presence than its three and a half inches of height would merit. In some lights it is pale brown, in others greenish gray. The upper surface of the bowl—a plate, really—is smooth, but underneath it is pocked by the quick, careless hand of the potter, showing the dark brown clay beneath and giving it that sense of country roughness so treasured in ancient Japanese and Korean pottery. It is beautiful always, but most beautiful when it cradles a freshly cut lemon or lime. We are not sure whether we grow lemons and limes because of it, or whether it is treasured because we grow them and it is their perfect container. However it is, that dish and the citrus it holds grace many winter tables here, whenever fish or schnitzel or any fried dish is served.

Though beautiful in itself, the dish, for all its precious antiquity, is not as startling as the citrus it contains, for one does not think of Vermont, with its almost legendary winter cold, as a place where citrus could be grown. And it is not, or is not in open ground, for all citrus suffers when temperatures drop below 40 degrees. Even *Poncirus trifoliata*, called Bitter Orange, the hardiest of the citrus group with eccentric spiny green branches that bear tiny sour, bitter oranges, will not really survive outdoors much beyond Zone 6. We know this because we have tried. But ironically it grows here in any case, as the most reliable understock for some of its most delicious relatives, the lemons and limes. Its roots take well to pot culture, and many citrus on their own roots do not, for they can be fussy about soil texture, pH levels, and watering. Oranges, at least in our experience, are hopeless, for whether grafted on *Poncirus* or on their own root, our summers are just not long enough to ripen a crop.

So we concentrate on a few varieties of lemons and limes, *Citrus limon* and *C. aurantiifolia.* They are all grown in large terra-cotta pots, stood outdoors in cool Vermont summer sunlight, and brought into the lower greenhouse in autumn. There, fruit formed the year before ripens through the winter, and toward the beginning of January, new flowers appear in clusters. They are five-petaled and waxy, with the incredibly sweet and tonic fragrance all citrus flowers possess. They are mostly white, though varieties of lemon show a reverse of pale burgundy. That is a color combination we find irresistible, and it occurs in other winter-flowering shrubs that share the sweetness of citrus flowers, such as the magnificent tender rhododendron called Countess of Haddington. Since the fruit of citrus clings to the tree for a very long time, one has flowers and fruit all at once, and even with that abundance, the overplus of shiny, dark green leaves. The leaves themselves are also fragrant, dotted over with oil glands that release a sweet citrus perfume when crushed. Oils extracted from the leaves are used by herbalists to treat anxiety and depression. We can attest to its efficacy, for on a cold winter day, when we feel we can spare a leaf, and we crush it and rub it between our palms, there is most certainly a lift of the heart.

Growing citrus in pots and tubs is hardly a modern innovation, and indeed, fewer gardeners grow them this way than in the past, where every gentleman's estate had its oranges, and many poorer people grew a plant in the cool, deep, sunny windows of a stone cottage, a rooted cutting "borrowed" from the estate. Citrus entered the colder parts of Europe as pot-grown plants sometime between the tenth and the twelfth centuries. The orangeries that resulted were the prototypes of the stove houses of the late eighteenth and early nineteenth centuries, and many fine examples still exist, at Versailles and even at Mount Vernon, where Washington built a quite elegant one, proof that when fresh lemons were served with tea and oranges after dinner, the young America did not lag behind its European origins in sophistication.

From a modern gardening perspective, eighteenth-century orangeries were fairly primitive affairs. However elegantly they were constructed, they were largely exposed to sunlight from only one side, and they were backed up under the foundations of a large palace, or in America arrayed along the sunny side of a barn or outbuilding. Heating was erratic, usually supplied by wood-burning chimneys and later by coal furnaces, but both were used only on the bitterest days and according to the alertness of the bothy boy, who slept in a loft above. Otherwise, the sun and its stored warmth did the work. They were dark and dank environments, unfriendly to most plants. But tubbed citrus are tolerant for the most part, and whatever leaves they lost in winter were gained back during their summer vacation outside as ornaments to the formal garden. They were usually planted in caisses de Versailles, the classic ornamental wooden boxes used there and still the resonant prototype for potting large citrus. Even in the less-than-ideal environments of the traditional orangerie, citrus produced a creditable amount of fruit, enough that Mozart on his way to Prague could stop at an estate and pick, peel, and eat an orange in the early spring sun.

Perhaps we do not have the skill gardeners possessed in Mozart's day. We are prepared to assume this, for even given the advances of modern horticulture, we have a great respect for the old estate gardeners and the knowledge they had. They knew how to force rhubarb and asparagus for the Christmas table, how to make strawberries bear for Easter, how to cosset the tenderest Muscat grapes, each one as big as a plum, and how to have ripe peaches in spring and salads all the year. We are spoiled now, because oranges are always available in supermarkets. But in the eighteenth century, a single orange in a Christmas stocking was a precious gift. Some of the knowledge the old gardeners possessed can be recovered. We have gotten so far at least as to produce our own citrus throughout the winter, thus returning the magic a single lemon or lime once possessed.

It surprises us that more gardeners living in cold climates don't grow their own citrus, for it is not very difficult to do, provided one follows the rules. Citrus, like African violets or many orchids, have exact and rigid requirements, and in that, they are just like folks. They demand a very open, airy, free-draining compost, for though they prefer to be kept evenly moist, they will not tolerate the lack of oxygen at their roots that results from gummy, waterlogged soil. It is therefore also important to have wide drainage holes on the bottom of the pot, and extra crocking. Pro-mix serves as an excellent root medium, though even it can be lightened with a little extra perlite and a few chunks of charcoal from the fireplace. We have found that stock grafted onto *Poncirus trifoliata* accepts pot culture more easily than do rooted plants, but if your own rooted plants are all you can get, take them. You will just have to be a little more careful with watering, which should be even and steady. If leaves cup and curl, the soil is too dry; if they drop off, probably it is too wet, or possibly temperatures have risen too high or dropped too low for the comfort of the plant.

Winter temperatures should be somewhere between 40 and 60 degrees, 50 being just about ideal. This may be the biggest problem in growing lemons and limes for home use. Few unused guest rooms or upper hallways offer these conditions, but in old houses, some do. The atmosphere around the plants should also be quite humid, a condition that can be maintained through frequent spraying with cool water, but is best if it is simply the natural environment in which the plant is placed. For most gardeners, a greenhouse is better. This will offer citrus the light they require to initiate their winter flower, and such an investment, if not economically wise, would certainly be emotionally so. In winter, citrus do not need much light, but they do need some. Six hours or so is enough. Insect pests can be a dreadful bother on potted citrus, though conditions toward the cool end of their range can discourage bugs. Otherwise, frequent sprays of organic insecticidal soap will hold down the problem until the plants can be stood outside, where natural predators will take over.

All citrus need a nice summer vacation. Perhaps, really, all houseplants do, even aspidistra, called in Victorian times the Iron Plant, for good reason. But for citrus it is crucial, and so pots should be stood in a sunny, warm place, away from drying winds, and with a little shade at the end of the day. People who think of citrus growing in the great sun-drenched areas of North America—Florida, Arizona, California—may be surprised that they do like a bit less light in the late afternoon, just when you might think of leaving the beach. Watering should be regular—neither flood nor drought—and a weekly application of a half-strength water-soluble fertilizer with a reading of 3-1-1—rich in nitrogen but weak in potassium and phosphorus—will encourage growth and fruit development. Citrus are also unusually particular in their need for trace elements: copper, zinc, magnesium, and others. It is worth searching out special citrus growers' mixtures and applying them according to recommendations on the package.

"But why bother?" critical persons might ask. "A lemon or a lime is only just something sour. It comes in bottles, after all." We'd have one sure refutation for such a comment, and that would be a freshly sliced Bearss lime in our special dish put on the table with a plate of Wiener schnitzel, produced from our own hand-nursed calf and dredged in beaten eggs from our own ducks. The lime is sliced only moments before dinner, when the main joy of homegrown citrus, their incredible perfume, is most intense. Whole worlds seem locked in an ovoid, greenish-yellow globe, waiting for release. Meyer lemons are as intense, more sweet, less sour, and if you slice one of each simultaneously, you'll feel like an old French *parfumeur*, blending two perfect scents into one.

In our garden, we do not lack for reminders that all gardening is improbable. It is, in Alexander Pope's phrase, "nature methodized," which is to say that much of gardening is cheating and tricks played on Nature herself, to make wonderful things happen in unlikely places and in unexpected seasons. So in winter here in Vermont, we will have a bowl of fresh camellias on the table in December, and in the howling winds of January, we will struggle through the snow to the lower greenhouse to pick a fresh lemon or lime, the fragrance of which, when cut just before dinner, will take us someplace else, as will the ancient Korean bowl on which its slices lie.

COWS

Even in a long life there are days—a few—in which the smallest details are not forgotten. We remember the day we met, the day we first saw this land, the day we moved into this house. And we vividly remember the day the cows came. The decision to keep cows is a momentous one, or at least it was for us, since we had never lived with anything bigger than a large dog. Cows can also be a commitment of years, even of a lifetime. We have neighbors whose cows have lived with their families since the 1800s. Generations of cows have followed one another as one generation of farmers follows another. Records have been scrupulously kept, so that cows dead a hundred and fifty years or more can be identified on paper, and so can the exact descent of the cows peacefully grazing in pastures today. Our own cows, now twenty-seven years on our land, are well into their third generation.

We keep Scottish Highlands, the oldest registered breed and one particularly adapted to life in Vermont. They are very rugged cows, capable of enduring bitter cold without suffering. Hence, they do not require a barn, and even resent one, refusing to go in. But of course they are also beautiful, not at all like cattle bred for milk, plodding, stolid beasts with great distended udders. Highlands are sturdy, swift, and agile. They are heavily muscled, with long shaggy coats, mostly red; noble, wide-spreading horns; and large liquid eyes framed by long eyelashes—what one can see of them, that is, for long bangs of hair hang between their horns, shading their eyes and giving them, for all their great dignity, an oddly zany appearance.

They came to us as a practical solution to a problem. Cows had grazed our woods and pastures for a hundred and fifty years before we came to own it. But they had been withdrawn for two years due to changes in ownership, and when we bought the land it had already begun to grow up in brush, sapling beech and maple and birch, and in sunny spots, thorny blackberry in sometimes impenetrable thickets. A sort of smudge had been wiped across the bases of the noble trees, and we faced either a degraded woodland or summers spent doing little else besides clearing brush. Neither was an exciting alternative to the beautiful gardens we wanted to make, or the tranquil strolls through shady woodland on hot summer days.

Kris Fenderson and Alston Barret, fellow gardeners across the river in New Hampshire, also kept Highland cows, half for their beauty and half because they keep down brush. We particularly remember their magnificent white herd bull (whose daughter we came later to love for so long), white being then a rare color in Highlands. Though huge bulls with long pointed horns seem to strike terror in people, he was a gentle beast, comfortable being admired and petted and willing to take apples from our hands. Though it had never occurred to us before, on the spot we made the decision to keep cows also. That year—1983—

was an expansive time in our life. We had just built a barn, so there would be ample room for bales of hay, fence posts, and spools of wire. We thought we might afford a small herd—or fold, as groups of Highlands are always called. But we decided to start slow.

A single cow, a nine-year-old heifer we named Daphne, came first, with a four-week-old nursing bull calf. Highlands are of two sorts: long legged and rangy, or blocky and close to the ground. Long-legged Highlands are American, having been bred to manage the deep snows of the upper West, where they are much prized for their endurance and independence. Daphne was one of these. Her coat was the typical rust red, and her principal beauties were a fine rack of horns and the thick, long bangs that covered her eyes. Despite her size, well over a thousand pounds, and her height, five feet at the shoulder, she was gentle and tractable. She arrived as if she already knew where she was and settled easily into her new life here. Her bull calf was a different matter, however. To begin with, he was no beauty, which is perhaps why the farmer who sold Daphne to us threw him in for free. He was also a willful child, slithering under the fences and showing up at dawn in our neighbors' alfalfa, for which he had a great appetite. He was actually the first cow we ate.

Our success with Daphne encouraged us to acquire our first herd bull, which was one of the most handsome animals we have ever owned. He was the son of the herd bull at Balmoral, the queen's own fold. Of course he had never seen Balmoral, much less the queen, since his siring was by artificial insemination. But he possessed by heritage a classic Scottish form, a massive blocky torso on short muscled legs and a broad, flat face. He was brindled, with red streaked with black. And he turned out in the end to be the most gentle and trusting of beasts. But his coming here was dramatic, traumatic, and finally comic.

We were concerned that his journey from the New Hampshire farm where he had lived would be as easy as possible. So we asked a farmer friend and neighbor if he would fetch him. Roy had worked with cows all his life, and Vanessa, his wife, was an accomplished horsewoman. We therefore assumed that our bull would be in good hands. But even the most careful planning can sometimes go awry.

Midmorning, he was loaded onto the cattle truck smoothly enough, and he arrived at North Hill just after lunch. It seemed a simple business to herd him the first fifty feet or so between the driveway gate and the pasture entrance. But the bull would not comply. Disoriented and frightened from the novel experience of a dark truck ride, instead of heading to the pastures he wheeled about and bolted for the woods across the road, where he immediately disappeared. So there was a bull, with horns, loose in Readsboro. And we couldn't find him. The woods he entered were dark with hemlock on steep terrain. After searching for hours, we realized that we needed help.

One of the pleasures of life in this simple Vermont village has always been the resourceful and hardworking young people. They have helped us from the first to cut wood, set fence posts, plow the ground, and weed the garden. At the time of our bull's delivery and escape, V. J. Comai, who had worked with us since the sixth grade and was now a junior at the University of Vermont, was still helping out when he could. Along with many other things, he was a skilled hunter, able to discern and follow even the faintest trail. For such a capable woodsman, the track of a fifteen-hundred-pound bull is not so hard to trace, though it had eluded us for half a day. It took him less than an hour to find our bull. But he was still loose, and skittish, bolting when anyone came near. But by a stroke of good luck, another young townsman, Chris Batchelder, had just returned from the West, where he had spent a year riding the rodeo. We asked him if he could rope our bull. It took him one try.

By then it was getting dark, and so we trussed the bull tight to a tree and the next morning drove to the vet for a tranquilizer.

We were given clear instructions, that the hide would be thick, that we really had only one chance, and that we should on no account break off the needle in the bull's neck. The sedative was prepared on our estimate of the bull's weight, which at best was approximate. And it turned out to be wrong.

At dawn, V.J. and Chris and many of our neighbors gathered (for of course the word had spread) while we sedated the bull with the intention of leading him up the road and to our pasture, a distance of about half a mile. The injection was successful—blessedly, no broken needle—and soon the bull began to grow sleepy. Gingerly, we untied him, fastened a stout rope around his horns, and began leading him to the road, where Chris Batchelder's wife, now eight months pregnant, waited in their jeep. The idea was to tie him to the jeep, which she would drive slowly while he trotted behind. For good measure, an elderly neighbor, Faith Sprague, had given us an old burlap sack, into which we had cut two holes to make a sort of bonnet to blind the bull's eyes.

But when we reached the road and before we could get to Mrs. Batchelder's jeep, the bull suddenly collapsed into a heap, sound asleep. Clearly, we had overestimated his weight, and the sedative was too strong. With great effort we got him to his feet, tied the rope to the back of the jeep, and Mrs. Batchelder began to drive. About two miles an hour was the best the bull could do, and that with a great deal of wobbling. Halfway up the hill, some idiot not of our village, in a pink-and-cream Cadillac, pulled up behind and began honking imperiously. That, as it happened, was a blessing, despite the rude gestures our young people turned and made to the driver. For it seemed to move the bull a tiny bit faster, and we arrived at our gate looking for all the world like an ancient pagan procession leading the sacrificial animal to the altar (except, of course, for the Cadillac). The bull slept for two solid days. And for all his life, we treated him with extra care, always giving him the first apples, to make up for the horrendous way he had had to enter our world. He was never again asked to do the slightest thing he didn't want to do.

He had come to us named Rusty, but we rechristened him Hadrian, after the Roman emperor, as befit his great dignity. Thus began the practice of giving Roman names to our cattle, which we have adhered to ever since. He and Daphne bore us many calves. Some we sold, some we gave away to neighbors, some we kept—Titus, his successor; Julia; Livia; and Pliny the Younger, who was Titus's successor, because bulls, unlike cows, do not live to a great age. Some we bottle-nursed for veal, and twice a decade we raise a bull calf for beef.

Organic, grass-fed beef is stylish now. Whole Foods sells it, as does Walmart. But in the '80s it was an exotic idea, considered by many farmers to be wasteful, as bagged foods, hormones included, and confined quarters occasioned much more rapid growth and weight gain. Highlands have little fat beneath their hide, their thick coats providing the warmth they require. Fed on grass and allowed free range, they never develop the marbling of fat preferred by most Americans. The meat is much more healthful and rich in flavor, but not butter tender, beautifully suiting the Italian and French preparations of beef we mostly favor, slow braises and stews and steaks grilled over the kitchen fireplace in the Florentine manner. And the cows lead active, happy lives to the end.

In the raising of animals for the table, we are deeply committed to home slaughter. Many years ago, when we lived in Pepperell, Massachusetts, we raised a pig named Morose, who had been given us while we still lived on Beacon Street in Boston. Her life was a good one, with lots of space to wander, and rich buckets of porridge and mashed potatoes taken from the leavings at a school for severely impaired children where one of us worked at the time. But in a year she grew from the cute little piglet we had had to keep in the bathtub on Beacon Street to a large and aggressive animal who was difficult for us to control. Her time was up. We took her to an abattoir for slaughter. That was not the way to end her life. She had been treated all her days with kindness and indulgence, only to be put in the back of a pickup truck, driven miles away, and housed in a concrete-floored pen with strangers. What happened next we try not to think of. There are things one does in one's life—too often out of ignorance—that remain there always, causing a wince in memory. The only remedy is to try to do better.

And so we do. Now we slaughter here, in spaces our animals are completely familiar with. We are very lucky in having a local farmer nearby who is a skilled slaughterer with a great knowledge of animals and compassion for their feelings. The other animals are always put out on the far pasture and the cow to be slaughtered is feasted on the best grass and apples until the moment of her ending. If we are to eat meat, we try to let as little suffering attend that as we can.

We are lucky, too, in our butcher, who lives on a barely passable dirt road in a rural community just north of Bennington. He has great skill at his trade, and our beef is dry-aged, hung for six weeks or so until it is crusted over but tender and flavorful within. Six or eight hundred pounds of beef is far more than two people can consume, even *with* guests for lunch, in a year. For even under the most careful wrapping and freezing, the meat's quality begins to deteriorate after that. So we have plenty to give to friends and family, and we barter it, too, for the game and wild salmon our country neighbors skillfully bag and generously share. It is never a pound-for-pound exchange, and very seldom does one package exchange hands with another. Rather, it is in the nature of a free gift for a free gift, from time to time, as one has something to offer. As such, it is a vital cement to a community already strong in its intrinsic values.

Coda alla Vaccinara
(Oxtail Stew)

I love oxtail any way it is prepared. In Jamaica they make a mean oxtail brown stew with butter beans, but this is how we prepare it in Roma.

The oxtail available on the market now is ready for cooking. When I lived in Italy the oxtail would be cut into pieces and left under running water for 2 hours or in cold water for 4 hours. Then it would be placed in a pot, covered with abundant cold water, brought to boil for 20 minutes, then taken out of the water. One more time it would be placed in a pot with cold water, sea salt, celery, carrot, onions, bay leaves, whole black peppercorns, a splash of white wine, and a leek if you want. They would let the oxtail boil for 2 hours, making sure to remove the foam as it was forming at the top. You can reserve this stock for the cooking of the oxtail.

And at this point the oxtail, patted dry, is ready for cooking.

3 tablespoons extra-virgin olive oil
3–4 pounds oxtail
1 carrot, chopped
2 shallots, chopped
1 medium onion, chopped
1 bunch parsley
4 garlic cloves, minced
1 glass dry white wine
2 pounds strained or crushed canned tomatoes
1 or 2 hearts of celery (just the white tender part),
    cubed
Ground black pepper
Sea salt

Some people add 3 cloves and a touch of nutmeg, but I do not. Others like to add pine nuts and raisins . . . I like mine pure. I like to use a terra-cotta braising pot, but use whatever you like.

Put 3 tablespoons of olive oil in a pot over medium-high heat. When it is nice and hot, add the oxtail (if you have boiled the oxtail with sea salt, you do not need to add any; if you are using raw oxtail, dust on all sides with salt and pepper). Brown the oxtail on all sides.

Add the carrots, shallots, onion, parsley, and garlic. Let the vegetables cook through, then add the wine and cook until the liquid evaporates. Add the tomatoes and 2 cups of hot water (or, if you have it, oxtail stock). Lower the heat to medium. Cooking time will vary depending on whether or not you have boiled the oxtail, from 1½ to 3 or 4 hours. Add liquid as needed.

Thirty minutes before the end, add the celery hearts. A good way to know if the oxtail is close to completion is by checking the meat close to the bone. When it pulls away, add the celery. Taste and adjust salt and pepper.

The result should be very saucy. You can serve the oxtail as an entree and use the sauce on rigatoni sprinkled with Pecorino Romano.

SERVES 4

From the kitchen of Beatrice Tosti di Valminuta

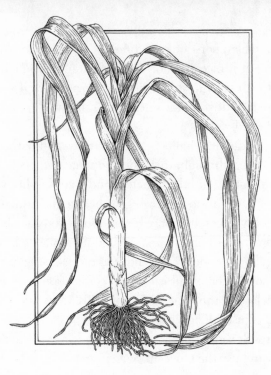

LEEKS

Leeks are the last thing we harvest from our garden. Indeed, we remember one dark frozen evening in November when the air was thick with belligerent sleet and the ground was crusted over with ice. We chopped our leeks out of the ground with hatchets, and the frozen earth clinging to their roots (one must keep the roots intact, for storage) made their weight almost unbearably heavy on our shoulders. But leeks are an important part of our harvest, the conclusion of a cycle that stretches from May to November, and reflect the discipline on which we have relied since we first occupied this land. To be a gardener, one quickly learns that not all garden tasks are pleasant, or done in pretty weather. So, frozen as our fingers were, there was simply no point in shirking the task.

Leeks are a part of the large group of kitchen alliums, and

like a gifted and clever family, all alliums have their special talents and distinctions. We would not be without a single one of them. Just as in families, some are stalwarts, ready to perform all tasks. Onions (*Allium cepa* var. *cepa*) are the most ubiquitous of kitchen vegetables, essential to almost every savory dish one can think to cook, to the degree that many weary cooks have pulled themselves out of their chairs saying to themselves, "Once I peel the onion, the rest will follow." Garlic (*Allium sativum*) might be argued to be the foundation of civilization, as a New York judge once sternly opined to a couple who had brought suit against a neighboring restaurant for the fumes that were emitted from its kitchen. It is impossible to imagine fine French, Italian, or Chinese cooking without its pungent bulbs, though one can imagine English cooking without them easily enough. Shallots (*Allium cepa* var. *aggregatum*) are really a subspecies of the onion itself, forming clusters of bulbs underground in their first year, as garlic does. But their flavor is far more suave than that of their sturdier sibling, and so they are the "onion" of choice for delicate meats and sauces. Chives are indispensable for summer cooking, creating almost a dance of onion flavor over omelets or vichyssoise, or even a plate of ice-cold sliced cucumbers dressed lightly with vinegar and oil. They are such pretty plants, in any case, with their rich mauve flowers throughout early summer, that clumps of them ought to be all about the garden. Prolific self-seeders that they are, this does not seem to be a difficult effect to achieve.

But of all kitchen alliums, perhaps it is leeks (*Allium porrum*) that possess the greatest aristocracy. For one thing, they are very beautiful plants, with strong central stems and great symmetrical, narrow flags of leaves, arranged in a flat plane and colored a wonderful glaucous blue, sometimes, in cold weather, taking on a blush of violet purple. The simplest onion in a row, its flattening bulb resting just on top of the ground and its tubular leaves standing upright, is a pretty thing in the gardener's eye, until it falls over, indicating that its year of effort is done. But leeks stand upright all their lives. This may indicate why they are the national emblem of Wales, where, in the sixth century, Archbishop David ordered Welshmen to wear a cleaned leek in their caps to identify themselves against the marauding Saxons, so that they would not be mown down by their own arrows. On St. Davey's Day, the first of March, leeks are always in short supply wherever Welshmen are concentrated. Leeks dug on that day would have stood in the garden all winter long, and that capacity is a peculiarity of theirs, since they are among the hardiest of all vegetables.

We take advantage of that hardiness as we go about harvesting more tender things. That happens in tiers, according to our sense of the autumn weather, which we monitor closely, both on our skins and through the radio and the long-range weather reports in *The New York Times*. When temperatures are expected to dip toward freezing—which now is late September or even early October but was late August when we came here—we bring in all the tender crops, the eggplants, peppers, mature beans for shelling before the fire, and tomatoes ripe and green, for the green ones will ripen stored on thicknesses of newspaper in the top of the stairwell, and we always assume we will get around to some jars of green tomato relish.

Carrots, beets, and celeriac come next, and they are often harvested with cold hands, sometimes in mists of snow, and trundled to the lower greenhouse to be packed in sand for long winter use. Most of the greens we let go. But if, on a mild late autumn day, we can rip away some fat collards or kale for a Japanese winter soup of rich broth, sliced onions and carrots, two fresh boiled eggs in halves, and some shreds of garden leaves, so much the better. We have special wooden bowls for this, each one turned from a single log. And we will hope to have a bottle of sake chilling in the snow.

A fat leek, cut lengthwise and then across, could be added to that soup. In leek and potato soup, rich with chicken stock, whole milk, and cream, they are of course one of the two main ingredients, though we also like to add at least one mushroom bouillon cube, imported from Italy under the brand name Star as funghi porcini and available from most good Italian grocery stores. Since leeks may be harvested at any time, we also make vichyssoise, that sublime American soup assumed by most people to be French, in summer. But for that, we like to add a whole cucumber, peel and all, to the final blending, the cool taste of which is a perfect undernote to the ice-cold soup. If small and tender, leeks also make a very good winter salad, either in combination with other greens or even alone. Remove the basal root plate along with the green top, and slice the cream to pale green bulb into narrow strips. Plunge them into ice water for 30 minutes, and they will curl, as does the Italian chicory puntarelle. Like puntarelle also, the dressing for the leeks benefits from a mashed anchovy.

But perhaps our favorite way of cooking leeks in the winter is as a braise, for then their curiously sweet and yet nutlike flavor is most apparent. The braise is actually completely similar to that used for early Egyptian onions or for scallions. Trim the leeks into even sections that will just fit a skillet in one layer, and quickly brown them on one side in butter, and then turn with a spatula to brown on the other. Add a cup or slightly more of good chicken stock, enough to come halfway up the side of the leeks, and simmer, covered, until quite tender. Remove the lid and quickly reduce the stock to a syrup, spooning it all the while over the leeks. Serve the dish as is, or sprinkle it with Parmesan and put it under the broiler until the cheese bubbles.

A braise of leeks is best made with slender stems about the size of a wooden spoon handle, and those are mostly what we grow, though a few larger ones are encouraged to develop for soups and stews. The cultivation of leeks is quite simple as long as two requirements are met: They need a deep, rich, fertile soil and abundant moisture throughout the growing season. Where irrigation possibilities are limited, leeks, celery, and celeriac should get the first rations. Leeks are also among the few vegetables that will accept some shade, as much even as half a day. Under these conditions they will not develop as large as our wrists, but since we never enter contests or hope for any other reason to show off great fat leeks, and since moderately-sized ones are most convenient for the kitchen, we are content with that. And as small leeks are our goal, they are set out quite close together, as close as four inches one from the other. Some thinning occurs for use in summer cooking, but mostly they stand close together until harvesttime in November. For vegetable gardens with limited space they are a boon, since their upright growth allows them to be intercropped with lower plants that develop earlier, such as radishes, lettuce, and other salad greens.

Since leeks are one of the first crops set out in early spring, seed should be sown quite early, no later than the end of March, quite thickly in mother pots, which are then set in cool, airy, sunny conditions to germinate and grow. Germination is often irregular, but the eventual result is a pot of fine green hairs, which, when transplant time arrives, are separated by swishing the whole mass in a bowl of water or running it under the hose. Care must be taken not to break or damage the usually single tiny, thickened white root. The plants should also be kept moist, perhaps in several thicknesses of moistened paper towel, until they are planted in the rows. But many nurseries now offer leek seedlings in trays of small plugs, and for many home gardeners, that is by far the easier way to go. Trenches are made about four inches deep, and each tiny seedling is firmed into place to stand upright. If a good rain follows, you will not lose a single one, for, like onions, leeks readily accept transplanting when quite young.

And then we arrive at the great debate: to earth up or not to earth up. The old gardening advice is to plant leek seedlings in deep trenches, as much as eight inches to a foot, and gradually pull the earth left in excavating the trench over the developing stem of the plants. The aim of this method is to cause the edible part of the leek, the white base shading into pale green, to elongate as much as possible. In itself it is a lot of bother, leading many home gardeners to give up on growing leeks. It also results in a kitchen problem, for inevitably some of the disturbed soil will find its way into the heart of the leek, necessitating that it be split lengthwise, fanned out, and washed for some time under running water to free it of grit. If you are aiming for the biggest leek you can grow, we suppose you might follow this method. Though it is extra work, the results will be perfectly fine in any recipe that calls for chopped leeks. But it is no good for braises, unless you tie the leeks back together with kitchen string after washing. The whole process might even make you reach for a package of frozen vegetables.

We never earth up our leeks, and we grow creditable ones, perfect for all our kitchen uses, which extend primarily throughout the winter, from November to April. Leeks are very easy to store, keeping quite well in the bottom of a refrigerator in bundles tightly wrapped in plastic and secured with rubber bands. If you are unsettled by touching slimy things, you may have some trouble with this method, since the outer leaves will become that way, creating a humid protective shield for the succulent inner core.

The solution is quite simple. If you do not have a place that is cold but above freezing, about 40 degrees being the ideal, buy a used refrigerator for little money and plug it in, in the garage or barn. Set it to a relatively low temperature and use it for storing leeks and perhaps other winter vegetables. You might also force a few pots of tulips or other spring-blooming bulbs in it. But even with this facility, don't hurry your harvest of leeks. The latest possible moment will give you the best keeping qualities, even if it must be, as it is here, in the sleet of a cold November twilight.

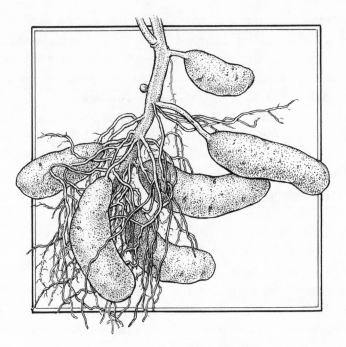

POTATOES

We have always been prey to enthusiasms. Never content with a little of anything, we have grown hundreds of species of primulas, antique roses by the dozens, magnolias by the score. So too with vegetables. We grow far too many varieties of beans, both bush and climbing, and never could we eat all the forms of chicory— puntarelle, pan di zucchero, grumolo biondo, Galantina—that we order from Seeds from Italy. Or even all the peas—Tall Telephone, Lincoln, Green Arrow, Caseload, Precoville—though outside pea season it is impossible to imagine the waste of a single pea.

Consider the beans. They come in an endless number of sorts, modern and heirloom, bush and pole. All have subtle differences—of ripening time, of flavor, even of uses in the kitchen, for though any bean not harvested fresh can be good dried, beans specifically grown for drying are a revelation, and there are many of them. And tomatoes. A friend has grown seven hundred fifty different sorts and written a book about them all. We have not grown so many, though over the years there have been perhaps a hundred. We could not count the number of lettuce varieties we have grown, either as standing heads or in mixes for scissoring as baby greens for salads, but they include iceberg varieties, so scorned by sophisticates but so good grown fresh and eaten from the garden. Each year, when brown envelopes of seed arrive from many companies, we wonder how we'll fit them all in. Somehow, we manage.

Not all vegetable families offer such temptation to excess. We have found no such great differences in celeriacs, now that the brown heart has largely been bred out of them. And for artichokes, though there are many we would long to grow, only one, Imperial Star, will reliably set bloom in our cold Vermont garden, where no artichoke will live over for a second try. Generally, soybeans are coarse and inedible, and so we grow only the few marketed as edamame, one variety of which seems identical to the other. But there are exceptions. Generally varieties proliferate as our enthusiasm for them increases.

Potatoes are perhaps the best example of all. Sturdy staples that they are, they can do a thousand jobs in the kitchen, and so, over the thousand years they were cultivated in South American fields, and the little more than four hundred they have been cultivated in other gardens, a thousand varieties have resulted. They differ in size and shape, color of skin, of flower and flesh, texture and culinary use, and most important, in taste. Once, twenty years ago—when the word "heirloom" was usually applied only to furniture and china—we gave over almost our whole garden to a trial of twenty potatoes, most of them unknown then, or very rare. That test ended up as an article in *Horticulture* magazine, and many readers were surprised to learn that there really is a difference between one potato and another, and that so many can be grown.

Many of the potatoes we grew in our Great Potato Trial have now become commonplace in markets. Yukon Gold was released only in 1980 but has since become the standard American yellow-fleshed potato, valued for its fine flavor and excellent keeping qualities. It is a handsome potato, inside and out, with shallow pink eyes on a smooth buff skin that is thin enough to leave intact for hash browns. Its flesh looks buttered before it has been. Because it is so readily available now, one might be tempted to forgo growing it, and this might be a necessary compromise if space is very limited. Still, one must remember that all compromise involves loss, for there is nothing quite like the crisp sound of a newly harvested Yukon Gold sliced on a chopping board. It is freshness itself.

Fingerling potatoes—which are in fact the length of a digit but swelled to an uncomfortable arthritic size—are also usually offered in good supermarkets. But they are not necessarily the fingerlings we most treasure. Rose Finn Apple came to us originally from Christopher Lloyd, whose favorite potato it was. It was the only variety he grew at Great Dixter, content to buy others for baking or mashing in the market. In that, we disagree with him, for even a Burbank Russet is better when harvested from one's own plot. But we do not disagree with his evaluation of Rose Finn Apple, for it is a superb potato. Long and narrow, it often has secondary swellings off the main tuber that seem fanciful beasts or even potato men, albeit men lacking a limb or having one too many. Its rose-blushed tan skin is yellow in color and waxy in texture. It makes an excellent German potato salad, boiled in its skins until just tender, sliced warm, and combined with a dressing of sharp vinegar and oil, salt and pepper, with perhaps just a sprinkling of sugar. But it's perhaps best boiled until tender, drained, and tossed in butter with fresh chopped parsley or rosemary (or both). What remains after supper makes an excellent cold breakfast, if not snatched as a midnight snack. We suppose cold potatoes are an acquired taste. We have it, here.

All of the fingerlings—and there are many—are essentially either salad potatoes or to be eaten whole, lightly boiled and then dressed with butter and herbs. One of them, La Ratte, is best eaten very small, of course in its skin. That skin is fine and netted, with a pale thread crisscrossed against the deeper tan. Potato skins are now common bar fare, usually made of some sturdy variety, such as Burbank Russet. But the home gardener should also concentrate on the more subtle pleasures of the skins of fingerlings, and especially La Ratte, which rubs pleasantly against the tongue as the creamy flesh dissolves. Of such refined pleasures is the growing of rare potatoes composed.

There is also the rainbow of colors in which they occur. Most fingerlings are buff or light tan skinned with yellow flesh. It is a pleasing novelty, though its flavor does not equal the red-skinned Rose Finn Apple. For really dramatic color, one must turn to Peruvian Purple, a cultivar (or several) that came into America during the '70s and seems genetically very close to the wild progenitors of all potatoes. The skin is near to plum in color and the flesh, cut lengthwise, is a startling blend of purple alternating with bands of watery blue, but if cut crosswise, shows an aureole of pale blue against deeper blue. All Blue is another popular blue potato, with blue skin and flesh. It is not a potato for boiling, since its high water content causes it quickly to turn mushy, and a blue mash or a blue potato soup, though intriguing ideas, will come to the table a most unattractive gray. The taste of most blue potatoes is also unpleasantly ferrous, and that, with their color, makes them seem odd. The combination is desirable in an oyster, but not in a potato.

The best of the purple-skinned sorts are those with white or yellow flesh. Purple Sun is one of the healthiest of all potatoes, and is especially rich in vitamin C and the antioxidant carotenoid. The skin is deep purple and the flesh an attractive deep yellow with purple streaks. It is wonderfully flavorful for roasting, and also stores very well. Purple Viking is handsome to look at, with deep purple skin marked with pink splashes and stripes; the flesh is bright white. We use it for baking, since it can produce very large tubers. But we confess that much of the pleasure of growing vividly colored potatoes does not always lie in their kitchen utility but in how their various hues look, washed and tumbled into an old, worn wooden bowl. People who grow potatoes quickly learn which are novelties, tried out for a year in the garden, and which are sturdy reliables, grown for various uses and for consistent flavor, year after year.

As late in the season as we dare, we therefore harvest two of our favorite potatoes, both excellent keepers. Green Mountain is an heirloom first released in 1885 in Charlotte, Vermont. But it is not local pride that binds us to it; rather, it is an excellent baking potato. One never need buy the seed of this potato here, for everyone grows it, and if one fails to put by seed, sprouted potatoes can be begged of a neighbor at planting time. The other is German Butterball, new to us three seasons ago, but our potato supplier, the Maine Potato Lady (www.mainepotatolady.com) says it is her favorite potato, and it has become ours as well. The tubers are medium-sized, with netted golden skin. The flesh is mealy, full of flavor but firm, and can be used in every way one wants to cook a potato: baked, boiled, or fried.

It is not hard to grow potatoes well. They ask so little—moderately fertile, acid soil that is reasonably moist, and lots of sunlight. But they must never be grown in manured soil, even if the manure is well rotted, for the results will be scab, an unattractive corky growth on the skins. Since skin is often a delicious part of any potato, scab must be avoided at all costs. So we feed our potato beds a manure-free compost, and sometimes turn a bale of peat moss into the bed in early spring. It helps, too, to plant scab-resistant varieties, which the ones we recommend all are. Colorado potato beetle, the only airborne pest we know, can be organically controlled with a strain of *Bacillus thuringiensis* specifically developed for potatoes. It is an organic remedy, and usually one application, when the beetles are first sighted, eliminates them all.

Potatoes are the only crop we grow here that is almost entirely for ourselves. Their spent tops are toxic to livestock, and so they go to the compost heap, where the toxins break down with rotting. The potatoes themselves are not palatable either, even to the pigs, unless they are cooked leftovers, and those we generally keep for ourselves. Still, we grow lots of potatoes, more usually than we can consume or give away. We would not call this greed, but rather a simple delight in abundance, in the plenitude of the garden that feeds us all summer and, with potatoes and other stored crops, throughout the winter and well into early spring. Never is that sense of abundance more felt than when the potato harvest has been good.

But nothing is ever wasted here. If we cannot eat all we grow, there are chickens and pigs and cows and geese with whom we can share our bounty. Indeed, the geese—brainy creatures that they are—begin a clamor if we have picked a single leaf of lettuce. And the two pigs, though they will eat every single shred of a bean or pea stem, will first root around for a neglected pod or two with audible pleasure. So come spring, as tiny piglets, they may actually also get the last potatoes, wizened and picked over but rough boiled to make them tasty. We even sometimes dress them with the stale butter found at the back of the icebox. Many creatures live here, and all must be fed as well as us.

WINTER HERBS

Winter's herbs are summer's herbs, too, but they seem to matter more in winter. Bay and sage, parsley and rosemary all grow here in winter in the protection of the greenhouses. Hardly a meal passes that one or another is not used to flavor a stew or a roast, an omelet or a soup. They matter in themselves, of course, their flavors redolent of warm days and places. But as much, it matters that we pick them. They come fresh from the garden when the garden—but for the glasshouses where they shelter—is covered in snow.

The quality of our winter harvest is very good, even from the giant parsley pot, which stands in summer near the kitchen door for ready picking but is trundled to the greenhouse below for use all winter long. We grow only flat-leaf Italian parsley, the seed of which comes from Seeds from Italy, which is now the

American distributor for the wonderful Italian seed company Franchi Sementi. For many years we grew the parsleys regularly available in nurseries, the curly because it is so pretty and the flat for flavor. Both served their functions well enough, as garnish and as something "green" in cooked dishes. But from a trip to Rome we brought back a packet of seed of Gigante di Napoli, and the plants that came from it were a revelation, deeper in flavor, parsley added to parsley. So we have grown no other parsley since that first experience. In a cool wet summer such as we often have, it does not bolt, but in a warm one we replant the pot in July for autumn and winter harvests.

The bay tree, with a trunk nine inches around and a formally trimmed head four feet across, was bought from Allen Haskell's wonderful nursery in New Bedford, Massachusetts, as a willowy, pencil-thin adolescent. For twenty-five years, it has lived in the same pot on the planted terrace outside the glassed-in winter garden. In autumn it is moved there, where it stands next to the two shallow steps that lead us from the kitchen into a tiny garden fragrant with the scent of tender rhododendrons and the improbable luxury of camellias to cut for the table. From our bay tree we harvest clusters of leaves all winter long—essentially, its annual pruning—but from so large a tree we can also give bunches away to friends, and must, since the pruning that keeps its head round and shapely must be completed by March, when new growth sprouts. But even that new growth, if we have been negligent, provides a wonderful, much more delicate bay fragrance to early spring dishes of asparagus gratins or creamed soups.

Sage, with its affinity for fatty meats and its traditional uses in Thanksgiving stuffing, is primarily a winter seasoning. Sage is a salvia, *Salvia officinalis*, in continuous cultivation for thousands of years for its believed medicinal powers, as *officinalis* always indicates. It can be had in fancy, variegated forms, golden and purple and pink-and-white-splashed leaves, but for the kitchen none is finer than Berggarten, which has typically sage-green leaves but much larger and rounder than the species. It is reliably hardy to Zone 6, and almost hardy here in a good year with snow cover. But we grow three plants in a large pot to provide the sharp drainage it absolutely requires and bring it under cover for winter use. Of all the winter herbs we grow, it is the least adaptable, because it thrives best in dry air and bright sun, conditions our winter garden and greenhouse really do not offer. But by feeding the pot heavily with slow-release fertilizer, we can produce abundant leaves in summer that we can harvest all winter long. Only the most pathetic growth follows what we take away, and by winter's end the whole pot presents a sadly plucked-over appearance. If we think it worth the trouble, we will transfer the entire root mass to the vegetable garden to regrow for summer harvests. But generally, it seems better to start with fresh, new plants.

Not so, however, with our venerable rosemary, which we have had for about ten years now, and which has grown to an impressive height of perhaps five feet. Of all the herbs we use, it is the one we turn to most often, since it is wonderful in all sorts of roasts—pork, lamb, chicken, and veal—and in slow braises and stews. Since we grow so much of our own meat here, it is nice to have our own rosemary as well. But we have not always grown it successfully. For many years we kept our rosemary in pots, summer and winter. Trained as decorative small, mop-headed trees, they were splendid stood about the garden as summer ornaments. But they were never with us for long. After a few years, usually five or so, they would begin to decline, dying out branch by branch until we had to discard them and start over, training up new plants. Then, about ten years ago, we decided to do a bedding scheme under the antique roses of the Rose Alley, a sort of Provençal display of lavender, dianthus, *Helianthemum*, *Centranthus*, and rosemary. The rosemary, transplanted from its pot into the open ground, grew vibrantly, far healthier in the garden than it had ever been. We found also that it could be dug up in autumn and put back into its pot. It never wilted, flagged, or complained but continued to grow strongly in the cool of the lower greenhouse and even produced its magical pale lavender flowers in late winter, which are wonderful in salads or as a garnish to cold dishes. So we have followed this practice ever since.

We prize this particular rosemary for its unusual richness of scent, flavor, and flower. We came upon it years ago in a nursery in Louisville, Kentucky, knew it to be special, and brought it home to Vermont. We have never happened on a finer. In winter, it occupies a clay pot twenty inches tall and about as much across, and in summer, we depend on the enormous strength of our young gardener, John Thayer, to muscle it from the lower greenhouse to the top of the Rose Alley (about a city block in distance) where it is replanted every year in the same hole, just at the turning of the path. Visitors always marvel at it and ask, "Can it be hardy in Vermont?" "By great effort" is the answer we have to give.

One other herb for winter use is of enormous importance to us but it is not grown here. It is oregano, and certainly we could grow it, and have. But our cool, moist summers, with abundant rain falling on rich woodsy soil, simply does not develop the intensity of flavor for which oregano is prized. For that, we have to turn to the arid slopes of the Mani, in Greece, where the parents of a young friend to whom we are deeply attached live, just above and in sight of the beautiful blue Aegean Sea. His father and often one of his visiting sisters make a day trip into the hills in high summer and bring back sheaves of oregano, which they spread out to dry in the hot Greek sun on the flat roof of their house. Oregano is unusual among herbs because it is much more flavorful dried than fresh, so the dry leaves are milled and sent to us, often in old jam jars with Cyrillic script on them. Our joke is that Greeks put oregano in everything, even ice cream, but Fotios's mother, who missed the joke, said, "Greeks never put oregano in ice cream!" Still, the power and the fragrance of the herb are so impressive that we include a pinch in almost every savory dish we cook, and certainly over the Sunday pizza.

For us, the garden and the kitchen have never been far from each other. So summer and winter and on every given day, one or more of these herbs will appear in some lunch or supper dish. There is hardly a savory dish that is not improved by the "handful of parsley" that so many recipes call for. So, in winter, we must remember to tuck parsley deep into the side pocket of our parkas to keep it from freezing, along perhaps with German Butterball potatoes in the other pocket, which, when boiled, will be so much improved by the addition of chopped parsley and, of course, butter. A cluster of bay leaves is the last thing put in when setting up a winter stew, along with a sliver of peel from one of our Meyer lemons or Bearss limes. Clusters always, for it is to be remembered that fresh herbs, though more delicate in flavor, are always weaker in strength than dried ones. Five or six single bay leaves might be laid head to toe over the top of a loaf of country terrine made from the liver, tongue, and other organ meats saved from the autumn slaughter, with ground veal and sausage, pistachio nuts, and lots of peppercorns, the whole dish spiced with good mustard and a "nipper" of cognac. When the terrine is cooked for its requisite two hours in a slow oven, the bay leaves on top contribute both flavor and beauty, turning a deep olive green when the terrine is brought to the table cold, sliced, and served with small green cornichons.

Sage leaves have more limited uses in the kitchen, though they are very important. Sage is strong in flavor, almost medicinal, but we treasure it just for that. Shredded into winter dressing for turkey, chicken, or pork roasts, fresh sage contributes a liveliness not to be gotten from dried and crumbled leaves. But our best use for it is perhaps in the classic Roman saltimbocca, a quick dish ("leap into the mouth" is the translation) in which bits of veal scallop—each one ideally about as large as the sage leaf that will cover it—are sautéed in butter and olive oil until lightly browned on one side, then turned with a spatula to brown on the other, the top side covered immediately with a sage leaf and a bit of prosciutto. Or in our case here, a shred of our own Canadian bacon, which is as thin as paper and fries up into wrinkled crunchy bits. Hot oil from the second browning is spooned over the sage and bacon to wilt the leaves, and when the batch is done—or batches, for you can do many at a time—it should be slipped into a slow oven to keep warm. The juices in the pot are then deglazed with a little red wine and quickly reduced, and the saltimbocca is put on a warm platter, the juices poured over. If you have a little chopped parsley from your parsley pot, that would be nice, too.

Except for our precious oregano, our winter herbs are all dependent on the fact that we keep two greenhouses, the winter garden off the kitchen and the lower greenhouse—really a conservatory—at the bottom of the garden. Without these facilities, a supply of winter herbs would not be coming to the kitchen. Nor could we maintain the splendid old bay tree and the rosemary that have been treasured occupants of our garden for years. Those facilities also offer us the possibility of stored leeks braised in the dead of winter, celeriac remoulade, forced Belgian chicories, carrots, beets, and potatoes always ready for winter meals. So, as we have before, we would make a plea for some greenhouse facility on the property of every serious gardener. The joys it offers are abundant. But none is more significant than being able to harvest one's own fresh herbs.

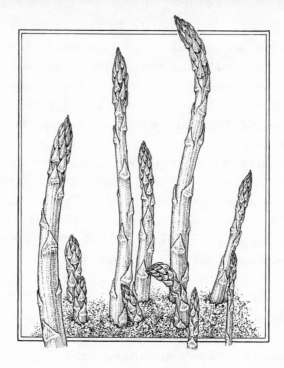

ASPARAGUS

In the spring of 1970 we moved from Boston to Pepperell, Massachusetts. We wanted to be rural people and Pepperell then was still a small village of long-settled families and working farms. The house we rented, built in 1759, was a tall white New England farmhouse that retained all its original features. It had small-paned nine-over-nine windows, wide pine floors, dark low ceilings supported by massive hand-hewn beams, and five working fireplaces. One, in the entrance hall just across from the front door, was massive, and still contained a wrought iron jack for hanging a pot and bread ovens to the side. There was one in the kitchen, one in the parlor, and one in each of the two upstairs bedrooms, which were connected by a wide glassed gallery that faced south. Seemingly endless land lay all about, for above the front house lawn was the town forest and below it was a wide meadow falling into woods. To the east were five hundred acres put into trust by the owners, and the west was a seldom-traveled road. We were two young men at the beginning of what would become a lifelong passion for country life. We could not have been more lucky than to start in that house.

Part of what came with this old farmstead was a long-cultivated vegetable garden, with soils deep from the manuring and tilling of generations, though when we moved in, the house had been vacant for two years and the vegetable garden was choked with pasture grass. It was spring, and at one end the weeds were pierced with vigorous thumb-sized spears of asparagus, hundreds of them in a bed perhaps forty feet long and five feet wide. As we were now the tenants of the house, the asparagus bed was ours to pick. And so we did, for over a month, an unjust vegetable reward for work we had yet to begin.

Some days later while walking along the road, we came upon an older couple who warmly welcomed us and introduced themselves as the Marshalls. Since the house we had rented was called the Marshall House, we realized that they had been its former owners. They were an old Pepperell family and, having inherited a larger house a bit down the road, they had sold it to our landlord. We asked them if they missed their old house, but as the one they now occupied was also "in the family," they were content with where they were. Mrs. Marshall did say, however, that she missed only one thing, and that was the asparagus patch. It had been planted fifty years before and had been in continuous production ever since. As there was more asparagus than we could possibly consume, we invited her to pick whenever she liked. And so she did, rewarding us with a beautiful, small, well-worn oriental rug that she could not find a place for in her new old house. We have it still. It was from Mrs. Marshall that we learned that we must cease picking by early summer if plants are to store up reserves for next year's harvest, and that we must manure the bed spring and fall, and dress it with salt marsh hay, the seed of which germinates only in coastal salt marshes. All that first asparagus bed asked of us were these attentions, which it abundantly rewarded. But years later, when we set out to establish our own first bed here, though we perfectly remembered Mrs. Marshall's advice about maintaining an established bed, for instructions about establishing a new one we turned to Thalassa Cruso.

Making Vegetables Grow was published by Alfred A. Knopf in 1975, a year before we came to North Hill. That first summer of 1977 it was constantly at our side, and to this day it is the first reference we suggest to those beginning a vegetable garden. Its general introductory chapters—on soil, organic matter, tools, seeds, pests, and disease—are solid and thorough studies of these things, as much as any good gardener need ever know. But it is the last third of the book, in which she profiles individual vegetables—beans, corn, cucumbers, peas, squash, etc.—that we find ourselves referring to in spring when we begin to plant our vegetable garden. Each entry treats of culture, harvest, ailments, and varieties. Some of the varieties have been superseded, though some have not. But all else is completely relevant, and the English Ms. Cruso, whom sadly we never met, had a vast firsthand knowledge of many branches of horticulture and a bracing, nononsense way of giving advice.

Her entry on asparagus was a bit daunting to gardeners in a hurry. She told us to prepare a twelve-inch-deep trench in autumn, dress the bottom with a six-inch layer of partially decomposed compost or manure and spade it in, leaving the trench open to the elements all winter long. (We learned an important lesson then, for one thinks one is adding a great deal of compost, but as it completes decomposition, it shrinks.) In spring, she called for 5-10-5 fertilizer, spread evenly over the bottom of the trench and covering that with unfertilized compost. Then the roots were to be spread out and set carefully eighteen inches apart and covered with two more inches of soil. As they sprouted, more soil was to be added gradually until the trench was full. The asparagus must then grow one full year without being molested, though it can be harvested lightly the second year and abundantly the next and thereafter. (At this point and after, Mrs. Marshall's advice served for the rest.) These instructions are detailed, clear, certainly labor-intensive, but they work. We followed them to the letter, and two years later we were harvesting basketfuls of asparagus. And then, we moved the vegetable garden. We did that five times, to make space for the ornamental gardens that were quickly developing until finally it came to rest where it has been for fifteen years and will stay.

In establishing that vegetable garden, we cannot guess why we took shortcuts with the asparagus, for Ms. Cruso had certainly proved her point. Probably we were impatient, for the site we chose for our final vegetable plot—a fine open space at the top of a meadow we had clear-cut—proved astonishingly labor-intensive to shape and level. Worse, it revealed itself as an ancient glacial dump; so many large rocks were removed from the space that we were able to build a four-foot-high stone wall at the edge of the woods above its east side. Perhaps the roots had come in the mail and the trench certainly hadn't been prepared the autumn before when that vegetable garden was still an unrealized scheme. And we are very sure that at that time it was one among many. In any case, the bed was a failure, never producing anything but slender weak shoots, "sprues," our old Vermont neighbors called them, which were worthless. Worse, it was three wasted years before we knew it.

The only solution was to tear out the bed and begin over, this time with Thalassa at our side. The second time we succeeded, one more case of "Do what mother tells you," because we thought of her as a wise but stern maternal figure, even from the first, when she launched her wonderful PBS program, *Making*

Things Grow, the same year as Julia Child's *The French Chef*, and back to back—a double dose of the two things we would come to care so much about.

Asparagus are dioecious, which means that plants are either male or female, and both are required to produce seed. Male asparagus plants are much more productive than females because they do not bear the burden of fruiting each year. All male strains are available, which must be the result of careful plant breeding, for we cannot imagine how one might determine the sex of a tiny wisp of asparagus seedling. Our present bed was to be an all-male affair, but in fact, a few females crept in. We have not removed them, for there is great beauty in their autumn gold stalks spangled with scarlet berries. Care must be taken, however, to weed out the abundant seedlings that will result, lest the bed become overcrowded. We have found little difference in flavor from one variety to another, and so our choice—as is often the case—has been aesthetic. Purple Passion makes purple spears that are beautiful coming out of the ground. But, like purple pole beans, the spears turn green when cooked.

White asparagus are considered a gourmet treat, and they were much preferred in the nineteenth century, we suspect in part because they looked pretty on ornate, highly decorated porcelain and were fancy. Also, you cannot tell just by looking when a white asparagus is overcooked, whereas an overcooked green one turns a most unattractive khaki green. White asparagus is not a separate variety but rather a plant from which all light has been excluded, either by earthing up or by the use of special forcing pots. At the busy season in which asparagus are harvested, the trouble of earthing up is out of the question. We do have forcing pots scattered about the vegetable garden, elegant terra-cotta domes with lids made by Guy Wolff. So we could produce white asparagus, but we never have. We prefer our asparagus green. Green, after all, is supposed to be good for you.

Asparagus has been grown since Roman times, and probably long before, as the great French culinary dictionary *La Nouvelle Larousse Gastronomique* says, *du temps immémorial*. Probably the best way to enjoy it is and has always been to boil or steam it and dress it with melted butter but, as centuries of gourmands have noted, asparagus has a particular affinity for eggs, either sauced in Hollandaise or quartered or chopped. The first-century gourmet Apicius offers a recipe for asparagus with songbirds and hard-cooked eggs. For good reason, songbirds are scarce in the kitchen these days (Apicius calls specifically for figpeckers), but his recipe for asparagus with herbs is interesting. It is a "patina," a very early version of the modern Italian frittata, and we repeat it here.

This recipe is very attractive to frugal cooks, for one always does wonder what could be done with those asparagus ends that normally get discarded. This is one solution, though two ingredients may be difficult for the modern cook to find. One is lovage (*Levisticum officinale*), a celery-scented perennial that most herb gardeners grow but can be scarce in the supermarket. The other is *garum*, a paste or liquid made from fatty whole fish packed into earthenware jars with strong-flavored herbs and layers of salt, topped up with the juice from green grapes and then sealed and left out in the hot sun to ferment until it is judged ready for use (about a month will do). Garum is ubiquitous in almost every ancient Roman recipe for a savory dish that has come down to us, rather as soy sauce is in Asian cooking. An acceptable modern substitute (if you are looking for a substitute; Pliny hated it) is the fish sauce of Southeast Asia.

It is very easy to judge the tastes of previous ages; doubtless our own will be judged by ages to come. And it is sometimes fun to recapture lost tastes, lost culinary practices. Still, before you set out your jug of fatty whole salted fish, herbs, and such, here is a modern adaption of Apicius's recipe.

(And then, there is always fresh just-harvested asparagus, a revelation when cooked minutes after harvest and dressed with salt, pepper, and melted butter. In season, even for Apicius, that might have been feast enough. It is for us.)

Asparagus and Figpecker Patina

Patina de asparagis frigdida: Accipies asparagos purgatos, in mortario fricabis, aqua suffundes, perfricabis, per colum colabis, Et mittes ficetulas curatas, teres in mortario piperis scripulos sex, adicies liquamen, fricabis, vini ciatum I, passi ciatum I, mittes in caccabum olei uncias III. Illic ferveant. Perungues patinam, in ea ova VI cum oenogaro misces, cum suco asparagi impones cineri calido, mittes inpensam supra scriptam. Tunc ficetulas compones. Coques, piper asparges et inferes.

Cold asparagus *patina*: Take cleaned asparagus, crush them in a mortar, pour on water, crush thoroughly, and strain. Put plucked and cleaned figpeckers [in a pot]. Grind 6 scruples of pepper in a mortar; add *garum* and grind; add 1 *cyathus* of wine, 1 *cyathus* of *passum*, and put this in a pot with 3 *unciae* of oil. Bring to a boil. Grease a pan, mix 6 eggs together with *oenogarum* in it, add the asparagus puree, and place it in embers. Put in the ingredients described above. Then add the figpeckers. Cook, sprinkle with pepper, and serve.

4 quail (or chicken) breasts
4 ½ pounds asparagus
6 eggs

FOR THE SAUCE
Ample peppercorns
1 tablespoon *garum*

1 tablespoon white wine
1 tablespoon *passum*
2 tablespoons olive oil
lovage, thyme, or other herbs

Figpeckers, songbirds with thin beaks, were considered particularly delicious fare by the Romans. Because they are obviously hard to find today, you can use quail or chicken breast in their place.

The recipe assumes that the plucked and cleaned birds have been half cooked.

Prepare the sauce. Grind the peppercorns and mix with the *garum*, wine, *passum*, and olive oil. Heat in a saucepan until it is well combined.

Boil the asparagus, drain it in a colander, then strain it through a sieve. Beat 6 eggs well and mix with the asparagus. Add the sauce and mix well. Pour this mixture over the birds and bake at 375° for 25–30 minutes.

This dish may also be served cold, as its Latin name suggests.

SERVES 4

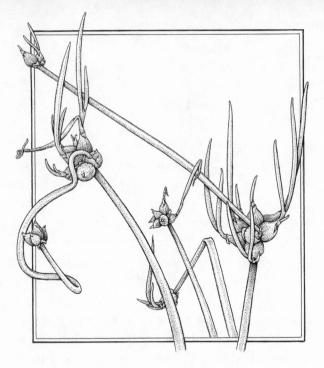

EGYPTIAN ONIONS

Years ago, we visited a garden that was unremarkable except for two extraordinary things—a snow white albino squirrel cavorting madly in the trees and an enormous bed of Egyptian onions, the stems bent to ground by the weight of their maturing cluster of bulbils. "What do you do with them all?" we asked. "Oh, nothing. We just think they are fun to grow." Many gardeners have agreed, and Egyptian onions are widely cultivated as novelties. But they have better uses.

Egyptian onions seem to suffer from an identity crisis. For one thing, within the vast onion tribe, botanists are not sure quite where they fit. Sometimes they are listed as *Allium cepa* var. *bulbiferum*, sometimes as *A. cepa* var. *proliferum*, and sometimes as *A. cepa* var. *aggregatum*. Even their common names are in confusion, for some gardeners call them "tree onions" and some call them "walking onions." All these names are descriptive, for the cluster of bulbils—tiny, perfectly formed onions sprouting on top of three-foot stems—look like a fanciful tree Dr. Seuss would draw. And when their mature weight causes them to fall to ground, they build a new colony at some distance from the mother plant, thereby "walking." Much like other plants—papyrus, for example—that share this method of propagation, they can cover a lot of ground, given the right conditions.

Of all their common names, we prefer to call them Egyptian onions, just for the exotic sound of it. But though onions were a staple of the ancient Egyptian diet, functioning almost as potatoes do for ours, whether the ancient Egyptians grew these curious plants is unknown. Even their origins are uncertain, though it was probably Western Asia, the Mother of All Onions, a fact commemorated in the domes of many mosques and churches. But as Egyptian onions reproduce from airborne bulbils, rather than from seed, for all their long history in gardens they have been pass-alongs, spreading throughout the world by clusters tucked into the saddlebags of ancient travelers or, these days, into the gardener's pocket. A great many of them have been sent out into the world that way from here.

Our own history with Egyptian onions stretches back over forty years, when we lived in Boston and tended a victory garden along the Fenway River. Sheer desperation caused us to do that—the hunger to grow our own food and perhaps also an inkling of what our eventual future would be. We had lived in Boston before, and then briefly as country people, and then had lived in Copenhagen and taught there. On our return to Boston, after a year away, we applied to the governors of the Victory Gardens, and got a plot. We realize with some smugness that we were ahead of our times.

Everything in Boston has a history, and the Fenway Victory Gardens are no exception. They are located between Boylston Street and the Fenway, a broad boulevard that snakes through the stagnant swampy marsh created by the aptly named Muddy River. It is perhaps the least glamorous part of Frederick Law Olmsted's scheme for an Emerald Necklace around Boston that included the Boston Commons and Boston Garden. Parts are actually very pretty, though other parts are choked with rushes, *Phragmites* principally, which make great thickets along its banks. This section of the Fenway is descriptively called—for reasons that do not perhaps require spelling out—"the Rambles."

But there is some high ground in this swampland, along Boylston Street, and during World War II the city made that section (along with parts of the Common and the Public Garden) available for the cultivation of vegetables to anyone living in Boston. It was part of the war effort, and it was a well-reasoned plan, since supplying the troops abroad had virtually eliminated fresh fruits and vegetables from the home diet. So all over America lawns were plowed up and vegetables planted with patriotic fervor ("Plant More in '44!"). Eleanor Roosevelt led the way, initially to strong objection from the Department of the Interior, by planting one on the White House lawn. When the war ended and California produce became abundant, most public victory plots were turned back to greensward and rose gardens. But once something takes root in Boston, it tends to stay. And so the Fenway Victory Gardens are still a feature of the old city, and along with the Dowling Community Garden in Minneapolis, share the distinction of being one of the few original victory gardens in continuous cultivation since World War II.

The Fenway Victory Gardens comprise about seven acres, divided into five hundred plots that measure approximately fifteen by twenty-five feet, though over the years these dimensions have become blurred, as owners have traded a piece of their plot for a piece of yours, or frankly "colonized" a bit of unused or neglected land. Though many of the small gardens are beautiful, the aggregate can only be described as homely. For in true Boston fashion, a minimum of control over the individual freedom of its occupants is exercised by the Fenway Garden Society. So along the paths that divide it, all kinds of human ingenuity have been exercised to mark off plots, from hedges of multiflora roses to driftwood to odd bits of posts and wires and other salvage. Still, it is a joyful place, where people exchange produce and give advice (solicited or not), small turf wars are fought, and democracy reigns, for on any given day the people tending their plots might be aristocratic ladies, essentially homeless people (more than one occupant has been known to sleep in his plot), wealthy young inhabitants of the Back Bay, or rural transplants to city life who just long for a bit of land to cultivate. We remember a dewy summer morning and a vast old lady who hoed her corn from a folding chair and said in her mellow voice, "Good Mornin'. This just like I be home."

Alas, when we gardened in the Fenway forty years ago, you couldn't keep a pig or chickens, and we are very sure you cannot now. But it was still, for two people who were temporary city dwellers, a vital connection with the land and with food produced by our own efforts. Or flowers, for when we gardened there, there was a remarkable planting of old roses, all meticulously tended. We remember walking to our plot, thinking *"Gruss an Aachen"* (Greetings to Aachen, Germany). That was our first introduction to what has become an enduring passion for old roses. And dumped along the Muddy River by some gardener who had had enough of them, there was also a thriving colony of Egyptian onions that had taken root in the muck. Throw an Egyptian onion anywhere and it will do that. We gathered some bulbils, and the plant has been with us ever since.

Egyptian onions are pure ease to grow. They are hardy from Zones 3 to 10 and thrive in almost any soil. They have no diseases, and propagation occurs simply by burying a cluster of bulbils in the earth, with its necks sticking out of the soil. But even if the cluster simply falls to ground, it will "take" and grow. They are fun, and children delight in them.

Many gardeners grow Egyptian onions as oddities, but they are vegetables after all, and though certainly vegetables can be grown for their beauty—as at Villandry, the great ornamentally patterned vegetable garden in France—generally our question about vegetables is, "How do you eat them?" So far, we have come up with a dozen answers. And with this versatile crop, we are not done yet.

Egyptian onions sprout in Vermont in early spring, long before the asparagus. Their crisp green blades of leaf that appear just as the snow melts signal a succulent feast. A clump can be dug, each shoot cut at the base and freed of last year's decaying slime. An excellent bunch of scallions results, ready to dip into salt and crunch, perhaps with a cold beer.

If you can resist eating them raw, you can make what old Vermonters call poor man's asparagus. This recipe is just as for leeks. Trim the scallions to even lengths and melt some butter in a skillet that will hold them in one layer. When the foam subsides, add the scallions, tops and bottoms neatly aligned, and let them brown on one side. With a spatula, turn them in one mass and brown the other side. Add half a cup of good chicken stock or white wine, and some pepper. Cover the skillet and simmer until the scallions are quite tender. Uncover and briskly reduce the liquid to a syrup. Serve hot, or to be really fancy, sprinkle some grated hard cheese over the top and put it under the broiler until the cheese bubbles and turns golden. The result is a beautiful gratin, perfect with a grilled steak or any roasted meat. You can also sauté bottoms and tops for an omelet, or for any dish that requires chives or green onions, such as a really fine macaroni and cheese.

There are also recipes for pickling the little bulbils, but that has always seemed a deal of work to us, what one might call a genuine "make use" recipe that would produce inferior results to the marvelously crunchy pickled onions one can buy in Asian grocery-stores. But if you like kitchen work, we pass on this suggestion.

Harvest the hollow round stems that bear the bulbils, pipe into them cream cheese seasoned with cayenne pepper, cilantro, parsley, whatever you like, chill the stems, and then slice them into rounds. Put each flecked cheese round surrounded by its pungent onion stem onto a cracker or toasted bread round, and top with three or so capers or a small pile of caviar. We think this is making a silk purse out of a sow's ear, but it is very good.

Egyptian onions have many undiscovered uses in the kitchen, and we wish we had had that knowledge when we visited our white-squirrel hosts. But here is a great caution: One cannot eat one's Egyptian onions and have them too. Always save a few mother plants, five at the least, to produce bulbils for next year's harvest. If you become addicted to them, you'll need more. And if you overindulge, you must simply beg a pocketful from another gardener, as, over the years, so many people have here.

It is an odd thing to live for more than forty continuous years with a plant. Our Egyptian onions must trace their lineage further back still, to whatever unknown gardener first cultivated them along the Fenway, and then dumped unwanted bulbils beside the banks of the Muddy River. How much further back they go than that is open to guess, for their history isn't well known. But they will persist here for as long as we are here, and we suspect—there is that determination to survive in them—a good while after.

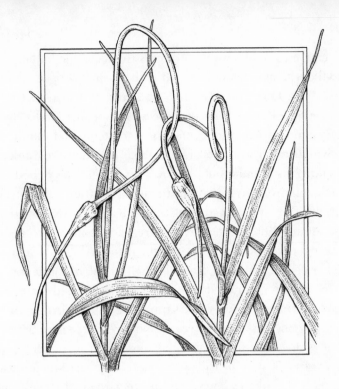

GREEN GARLIC

Garlic lovers—and they are legion—will perhaps be very disap-
pointed in us when we say that we have little interest in growing
garlic to harvest for winter storage. That is not because we don't
use it, for we do with a liberal hand—in soups and stews, in pasta
sauces and shrimp dishes, and sautéed in olive oil with green leafy
vegetables, such as escarole, chard, or kale, the cloves numerous
and left whole, equal players in the dish. There are hundreds of
garlic varieties, many of them heirlooms of long lineage and associated with specific garlic-loving cultures: Poland, Germany,
Italy, France, Spain, Korea, China, and Southeast Asia (not so
much England or Scandinavia, except among gourmets). There
are also garlic connoisseurs, who endlessly test and comment on
newly discovered garlics, discriminating between "hot" and "bit-

ing" and "mild" and "sweet" and "lingering" (as perhaps on the breath of your neighbor at a concert?). We wonder how they do this: Do they bite into cloves raw, or simmer them in olive oil until a bit gentled and tender? And when your tongue has been whisked over by one garlic, can you cut fine hairs between it and another, or several others?

We confess that unless we come across a head of garlic that is musty with age, we cannot discriminate much between one and another. Some are easier to peel, it is true, and we search out those at good markets, knowing almost by looking which are which. Heft, and a firm pressure between thumb and forefinger can also tell you whether a garlic is fresh or stale from storage. If it is firm and hard, it is probably fresh enough. And if ever the skin, white or purple streaked, is spotted with black dots, pass that garlic over, for its skin is surely infected with mold, which will impart that taste to the garlic itself. Beyond this, we confess we can discriminate very little between the taste of one head of garlic and another. That is in part perhaps because we never use it raw but as an ingredient of slow-cooked stews and braises, or tamed of its harshness by sautéing it until it is pale gold in olive oil, just to cover, in a tiny cast-iron pot perfect for that purpose.

Still, however, we have never accepted the comment that something should not be grown in the home garden because you can buy it in the supermarket, or the local farm stand, or the Saturday farmers' market. The whole argument of this book is that growing one's own food (or as much of it as possible), nurturing it, harvesting it, admiring it, and storing it and, most particularly, knowing what best to do with it at its various stages of maturity, are all vital learning experiences, for as surely as the preparation of a familiar dish always teaches you something new, the growing of any vegetable results in a greater awareness of its cultural requirements and in better uses of it at the table. There is also the indisputable joy of being able to say about a fine basket of ripe tomatoes or shelled beans or a tumble of celeriac roots: "I grew that!" It is a childish pleasure, equal to a boy holding up a full string of trout, or children who spent a whole morning berrying and return with juice-stained lips and pride carrying galvanized buckets full of soft, shining fruit. Both come from the vital human need to see connection between labor and achievement. We are very sure that a large basket of plump pods of garlic, brought from the garden with outer papers silvery white or richly streaked with purple, would give us a fine sense of pride.

And it may yet, someday, for we are sure that committed garlic lovers will say we proceed out of ignorance, and we know that we contradict the argument we made for growing one's own onions. But for the moment, our plot has many claims on its space, and growing garlic for pods has lost out in our greed for peas and fresh tomatoes, artichokes, beans, essential root vegetables, and a host of leafy greens.

That is not to say, however, that we do not grow garlic at all. It is one of the most treasured of the midspring greens, for we take it as green garlic, just when the shoots have gotten sturdy and the root is still a single small bulb, the whole looking like a slender scallion. Green garlic has dozens of uses in the kitchen, to the point that its harvest amounts to an eagerly anticipated small festival. We eat it chopped into scrambled eggs or in an omelet, we pound its tender leaves and shoots in a mortar and mix them with unsalted butter for a gentle garlic spread, we use it as seasoning for any white stews such as chicken or veal, and it is wonderful with fish of all kinds. In all these dishes, the flavor is recognizably garlicky, but also mild and sweet, never assertive or overpungent.

But perhaps the very best use of green garlic is on top of the Sunday pizza, since we fully adhere to a remark once made by Sophia Loren that "Sunday without pizza is a week lost from your life." Loren is Neapolitan, of course, and so she wants a rather thick pizza, in which the crust is not a thin little piece of cardboard designed only to hold the ingredients above it, but a substantial bread, the crusts of which are always eaten and relished.

Sunday Pizza

The dough is easy to prepare using a sturdy mixer with a bread hook, though many people still do the mixing by hand in the traditional manner and with great results. Here, we use a KitchenAid, forfeiting a certain romance, to be sure, but keeping ourselves from utter distraction with guests clustering around. Here are our instructions for two generous pizzas. Amounts are approximate, depending—as all good cooking must—on feel.

FOR THE CRUST

    3 packages dry quick-acting yeast
    1½ tablespoons sugar
    4 cups all-purpose flour
    4 cups bread flour
    1 teaspoon salt
    ⅓ cup + 2 tablespoons olive oil

FOR THE TOPPING

The ingredients will vary according to the season and what is on hand; there is almost no limit to possible combinations. You could, for instance, smear onion confit as a first layer, then thin bits of fresh mozzarella, thin slices of prosciutto or hard salami, then a sprinkling of pitted black olives.

For spring pizza, it is generally best to limit the toppings to not more than three, with the last being sprigs of green garlic crisscrossed over the other toppings. That does not include, of course, dried oregano and fresh-ground pepper.

In summer, it should go without saying that the top layer is paper-thin slices of fresh tomato.

In all seasons, scatter freshly grated Parmesan cheese over the top and, finally, the obligatory dribble of olive oil, concentrating especially on the edges of the crust so they won't be ignored.

Heat 1 cup of water to around 115° and pour it into a small porcelain bowl. Sprinkle the yeast over the top and, over that, lightly dust ½ tablespoon of the sugar. Soon the yeast will begin to sink to the bottom and start to foam.

Meanwhile, in the large bowl of the mixer, combine the flour, salt, 1 tablespoon of the sugar, and ⅓ cup of the oil. Add the foamy yeast mix and about 2 cups of warm water.

Using the dough hook, blend the ingredients slowly until they come together in a mass. You may need to scrape down from the sides of the bowl with a rubber spatula. Turn the mixer to medium-high. If the dough seems too sticky and soupy, add more flour. If it seems too stiff, add water, 1 teaspoon at a time. Most of the dough should be rising up on the dough hook, not puddling at its base. When the dough seems to be moving as one mass, continue kneading until it is smooth and elastic.

In a large earthenware bowl, place 2 tablespoons of oil. Turn the dough into the bowl and slide it around and flip it over so that the entire mass is covered with oil. Cover the bowl tightly with cling wrap and set it in a warm, draft-free place to rise until double in bulk. This should take about 2 hours.

Punch down the risen dough to deflate it. Divide it in half, press it into two tidy balls, and dip them in the flour to coat them. Place them on well-oiled standard pizza pans and let the dough rest for 5 minutes. Then press it gently out to the edges of the pans.

While you are waiting for the dough to rise, about half an hour before you expect it to be completely risen, assemble the ingredients for your toppings (which, of course, do not have to be the same for both pizzas). Preheat the oven to 400°.

When the pizza is assembled, pat it down lightly with your

hands. Cook until the topping is bubbly and the crust is a beautiful golden brown, about 45 minutes.

It is a huge help to have a pizza wheel to cut apart the pieces. Kitchen shears will also do an excellent job. Serve immediately.

MAKES 2 EIGHT-INCH PIZZAS

Most garlics bought in supermarkets are varieties of *Allium sativum*, which reliably produces large, satiny, often pink-striped heads with large cloves. But the variety we grow for green garlic belongs to the rocambole clan, *Allium sativum* var. *ophioscorodon*, many varieties of which have been identified over centuries of cultivation. The rocamboles are easy to distinguish from other garlics because in early to midsummer, individual plants produce pencil-thin stems surmounted by rounded scapes above their two-foot-tall dark green strap-shaped leaves. Those scapes, pointed at the end, will begin to loop and curve into fantastic but graceful patterns, which are a delight to children. Many gardeners sever them to increase the yield of the bulbs. But they still have their uses, for gardeners/cooks stir-fry them in mixed greens, and flower arrangers dry them for their fantastically antic curls. Because of this trait, they are sometimes called Serpent Garlic. If they are allowed to remain on the plant, however, they more or less straighten up, and the pointed, protective sheath turns papery and sits on top of a dozen or more little bulbs for a time like a jester's cap. Each bulbil is capable—in three years or four—of producing its own scape, and possibly a useful garlic bulb.

Rocambole, unlike most supermarket garlics, is fairly picky when it comes to growing conditions. All garlics relish a deep, rich soil, perfect drainage, and plenty of moisture. Most benefit also by side dressings of fertilizers or composts throughout the summer. But most commercially grown garlics resent winter wet and cold, which either inhibit the development of a root system between autumn planting and the onset of cold weather, or cause them to rot in the ground. Rocambole, in contrast, is much more tolerant of cold, wet autumn soils and of long, cool springs, which it relishes. Hence, it has always been the garlic of choice for Poland, Germany, middle Europe, and northern Italy. There are a wealth of forms to choose from—Polish Carpathian, German Red, Killarney Red, Amis Rocambole, Purple Italian, Korean Red, and Spanish Roja. We confess that we do not know the actual identity of our own. It was bought as a handful of rather small heads years ago at the Union Square Market in New York, from a harried young woman to whom we explained that we wanted it for growing. She really wanted her produce to be understood and her efforts appreciated. "Do you *know* how to grow garlic?" "Well," one of us replied, "we think we can figure it out."

We haven't had to figure much. For once the handful we bought was carefully separated and planted in a row of the vegetable garden in October, they sprouted in June, and even in that first year we stole a few for the kitchen. We know to curb our greed so that a certain portion of plants will always be left to produce tiny bulbils that fall to ground and sprout. They show in early spring as tiny green hairs around the mother plants, and they may be transplanted into a new row that will produce green garlic shoots for harvest the following year. It seems we may never have to buy stock of rocambole again.

Late each winter, we spend hours at the kitchen table with piles of seed catalogs, searching for old varieties we have loved for years and giving careful attention to those that are "new and improved." The seed we choose may be heirlooms, vegetables whose cultivation can be traced back a hundred years or more. Or they may be vegetables we never thought to grow here, like Imperial Star artichokes, which give us the pleasure of their ripe chokes far from the California bluffs where they grow best and offer an improbable grace to our late summer table. All this is joyful work, a place in which the dreary snows of winter and the new sun of spring seem to join hands in the mind and be one.

But no garden crops give us greater pleasure than those that, having been planted and given the right conditions and paid mind to, just simply return, year after year. Asparagus certainly fits into this group, and rhubarb. Horseradish, in a fine variegated form, returns each spring to the corner it occupies, and we like looking at it, though we have yet to make our own horseradish sauce. But it is perhaps Eygptian onions and green garlic that make us most aware of the continuity of our vegetable garden. Their steady persistence each spring prepares us with cheer for the season's work ahead.

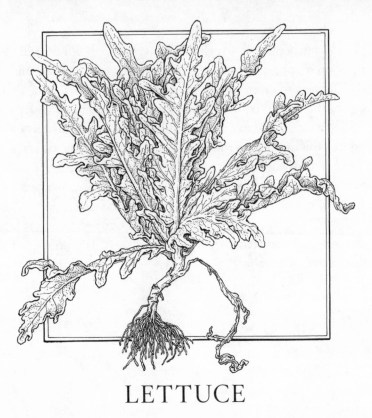

LETTUCE

Perhaps, if our vegetable garden had to be reduced to one crop—or even to a window box—our choice would be lettuce. We'd passionately miss other things and we would be desperate about a lack of fresh peas, perhaps our favorite among all vegetables in their brief season. But to us lettuce is like bread. It is the foundation of every summer meal, and the salad bowl is hardly dry between lunch and dinner. Lettuce is the only vegetable we can eat day after day and never tire of. Like boxwood in the garden, one can never see too much of it, or too often. Occasionally, other ingredients get thrown in—a sliced cucumber, perhaps, some young spinach or chard thinnings, a very young green onion chopped fine—but mostly, lettuce stands alone, lightly dressed and tossed, not shredded but as whole leaves. When guests are not here we eat them with our fingers, leaf by leaf. Raw garlic is never admitted to a lettuce salad, because then all one tastes is garlic, and the taste of lettuce is rich in itself, or many richnesses, if one learns to discriminate.

With many vegetables, after some years of experimenting one settles down to two or three varieties, trying an occasional new one just to vary routine or because an exciting new catalog comes one's way. But the thing about lettuces is that there are hundreds of desirable varieties. New offerings, either heirloom or modern forms, appear with every winter seed catalog. This plethora of choices can be either exciting or frustrating, depending on one's bent. The exciting part is that there is always something new to try. The frustrating part is that sometimes a variety one has liked seems to have morphed into something else, with a new name and new promises of excellence. Even the sturdy old iceberg, for example isn't just "Iceberg," as one would hope and expect. It can carry a dozen names, under "Iceberg Types."

"Types" are perhaps the best way to proceed with lettuce varieties, and it is the approach adopted by the ever-sensible Johnny's Selected Seeds. Leaf lettuces come first, and it is reassuring to find the redoubtable Black-Seeded Simpson among them. We would not be without it, for it is sturdy, reliable, quickly forming loose, mature heads in about fifty days from direct sowing at any time during the growing season. Like all loose-leaf lettuces, it tends to form floppy, lax crowns that never firm up into anything like a Romaine and certainly not an iceberg. Consequently, leaf lettuces lack the satisfying crunch of either. But they may be harvested as young thinnings, and later, as individual leaves from still-productive plants, and eventually, when signs of bolting begin to occur, as whole heads. Within the leaf lettuces are the Oak Leaf types, which form beautiful lobed leaves too fragile for general shipping and so are reserved as a luxury of the home garden. Particularly wonderful are several red leaf, for though their taste and texture do not vary much from the green, their vivid maroon or maroon-tipped green leaves are a visual addition to a salad. All leaf lettuces, being light and filmy of texture, are very easy to overdress. A light vinegar and oil does it; they are not candidates for creamy blue cheese.

Romaine lettuce, often listed as Cos, or Kos, is perhaps best for that. It has an interesting history, for, like many lettuces, it is of very ancient lineage. It was first grown by the ancient Egyptians, in a form we can recognize from tomb paintings, though it appears to have been a very tall plant, perhaps to three feet. It was taken up by the Greeks, who passed it on to the Romans. Lettuce has always been assumed to have therapeutic value as a sedative and pain reliever, perhaps because its milky sap so much resembles that of the opium poppy. In fact, before the invention of ether, it and inebriation from strong spirits were about the best things available for the excruciating pain of serious operations, eighteen heads being the usual pre-op dose. (Eaten in excess, lettuce has always been believed to stimulate sexual desire—and poor performance.) Lettuce seed was exported during the Renaissance from the Greek island of Cos, famous as the Isle of Healing, where the Asclepeion was located, in which Hippocrates is said to have trained. The most famous hospital of the ancient world, it functioned for a thousand years. Lettuce from Cos was grown in the papal gardens in Rome and hence became known as Romaine, a name that has prevailed in America, though the more ancient one, Cos, is used in Britain.

Romaine lettuce forms an outer circle of several layers of loose leaves and eventually tightens to an oval tight-packed core that is self-blanching so that the inner leaves are pale green, crunchy, and sweet. If we have plenty growing, we throw all the outer leaves to the geese, though a few of them might end up as last-minute additions to a bowl of Japanese noodle soup, or perhaps tossed into a mix of other, stronger and more bitter, greens, sautéed with garlic and oil to make what Greek cooks call *horta*. But the inner leaves are best and will stand up to a thick cheesy dressing, if one is craving that, but are probably still best when lightly dressed with vinegar and oil. This is the lettuce that is nicest eaten with one's fingers, and one can perhaps make a ritual of it, dipping each leaf into a bowl of well-seasoned dressing on the side. Red forms are available, and they are nice for color contrast, but we have not found them equal to the sturdy green types, either in flavor or crunch.

Butterhead, sometimes called Bibb lettuce or Boston lettuce after that proud old city, are aristocrats within the lettuce clan. They form small, tidy, and very beautiful rosettes on the ground and for perfect development should be given a more ample spacing than other lettuces, perhaps as far as ten inches plant from plant. The outer leaves, in a loose ruff, are still succulent, but it is the creamy, buttery head one really wants. If plants are grown in clean, sand-free soil, or perhaps mulched with hay, the individual heads are best served quartered, so that one gets all the experience of texture from the outermost green leaves to the pale gold centers. Some lettuces are best at the beginning of a meal, and some with it. A good Boston lettuce is perhaps most delicious after the main course, when each diner can put a lightly dressed quarter on his or her plate and "marry" it to a remaining bit of some rich sauce or gravy. Again, there are red and red-splashed forms of Boston lettuce available, and though they are interesting in the salad bowl, they do not seem improvements on the pale, greenish ivory of the traditional form. But among Bibb lettuces are forms of Deer Tongue, which make leaves that are pointed rather than rounded. Like Oak Leaf lettuce, they are too fragile for shipping and so should always be grown in the home garden.

The Batavia lettuces, sometimes called French Crisp or Summer Crisp, are all midseason varieties that will accept some warm weather without bolting to seed. They are a midway group between loose-leaf lettuce and Romaine, since their outer leaves may be harvested selectively, one from this plant, one from another, and then left to form heads that are not as crisp and dense as Romaine lettuce but still very nice in the salad bowl. In our experience here they tend to be a bit leathery and chewy, which probably means we have been stingy with the geese and not given them their fair share of outer leaves. A row of lettuces in neatly spaced ranks is always a challenge that way. It is hard to interrupt the even march to take a whole head.

Then there is iceberg lettuce, which is in an odd class of its own. All gardeners know how deeply debased a wonderful garden crop can become. Given the preciousness of peas, for example, how did all those peas get into cans? Or string beans? Or pickled beets? But no good thing has ever been more debased than iceberg lettuce, known best, and most maligned, from its use as limp leaves on hamburgers and watery components of bad restaurant salads combined with underripe tomatoes. Actually, however, when grown in the home garden and harvested fresh, it can be a revelation. It is also very beautiful in the garden when spaced far apart to give it room for full development. Then it forms handsome symmetrical heads, the outer leaves neatly arranged and frilled at the edges, the inner ones folded in onto a tight ball. We went to a dinner party where, among starched linen and pretty china and silver, a single perfect head of iceberg lettuce formed the centerpiece, sitting in a fine old mossy clay pot. That is not the way one generally finds it in the local diner.

So rich are the offerings of lettuce that we confess we grow only a few from direct sown seed. Mostly, we depend on Walker Farm in nearby Dummerston for perfectly grown little plants of many varieties, cute even when they arrive, each in its own two-inch pot. As we turn the rows of the garden in early spring, we plant two beds of them on either side of the central path. Each is five short rows across, and we mix up the colors and forms, planting now a red one, now a Romaine, now one with green leaves specked with burgundy, and now a Boston, to form a sort of tapestry. They develop quickly, and we plant them a little more closely together than one might, in order to take every other head and still not destroy the beauty of the planting. When the whole first rows are cleared, we plant them with bush beans or other crops, and move elsewhere in the garden with flats of new lettuce seedlings.

We do sow many lettuces from seed, but they are generally not for growing on as individual heads but for harvesting as baby greens, using scissors and cutting about an inch above the growing crowns, in order to secure a second crop, and sometimes even a third. Many mixes of mesclun, or *misticanza*, are available from seed houses. Some are only lettuce, and some are mixed and include mustard and arugula and other pungent greens. They are all sown in drills made by marking a straight line with a bamboo pole and then widening it with a scrape and a press of the palm to a hand's width. Seed is sown rather thickly, and if there is a bit of seed left in a package of Black-Seeded Simpson or Merveille des Quatre Saisons, it is shaken up in the mix. The wide drill is then scattered over with crumbs of fine soil, barely covering the seed.

By transplanting and by direct sowing, we manage to have lettuces in some form or another from late April until the end of October. No other garden crop gives us quite so long a span of harvest, and so it is a good thing that lettuce is such a staple and that we tire of it only when we have had enough of it fresh from the garden, which is almost six full months. We know people who keep it going in cold frames throughout the winter, for there are forms of lettuce that are very hardy. We also know some who grow a few wan leaves in home greenhouses, more content, perhaps, with the idea than the reality. But by the beginning of October, we are glad to turn to winter salads, of celeriac and carrots and beets. When they are gone, it is time to be hungry for lettuce again.

OLD HENS

We have always kept chickens. We kept them our first year together when we lived on Beacon Street in Boston and let them wander about on the parquet floors. We kept hundreds during the two-year idyll we spent on a five hundred-acre farm in Pepperell, Massachusetts. But it was not until we came to Vermont that we began to eat them. Like so many of the country habits we adopted, raising chickens for the table was a completely serendipitous decision.

Along the Colrain Road that connects our little Vermont town with the great world beyond, Greenfield and Northampton and Boston and New York, are many farms. They are largely cattle farms or hay farms or farms given over to the raising of field corn. But one day as we passed a dairy farm we had passed a hundred times before, a small hand-lettered sign stood in front of the house offering OLD HENS. We did not even need to ask each other but pulled the car into the driveway. The old farmer, old to us, at least, though he was probably only forty-five, told us he had a flock of Rhode Island Reds, healthy birds, but now four years old and laying fewer and fewer eggs, not enough to justify their feed. There were twenty-five in all and we bought the lot.

Once we had them housed in the barn, we were surprised at how many eggs they did produce, not twenty-five a day, but five or six, at any rate. Still, we tried always to keep to our intention and that had been from first sighting the sign to eat them.

The killing was simple enough. We wrung the neck, breaking it instantly so the animal died quickly. But then came the plucking, and here our naïveté was painfully evident. Irma Rombauer in *Joy of Cooking* had taught us to first singe the dead bird in a cauldron of boiling water, after which she promised the feathers could easily be pulled from the skin. They couldn't, though, for although those instructions work perfectly well with young birds, these old hens were as tough as the boots on our feet, and for every feather we extracted we pulled with it a piece of skin. Clearly, were these birds to be of any use at all, we would need to forgo plucking and skin them as we would a deer or cow.

Skinning a bird is ease itself. All one need do is make a clean cut from the neck to the tail along the breast deep as to touch the bone. The skin can then be pulled back as easily as the skin of a banana. The only innards we eat are the livers, which we prize, but we put the hearts and gizzards into stocks. For stock is the fate of any old hen; stock or perhaps, after many hours of simmering on the stove, a meat pie. But such a stock or pie really depends on truly old hens, birds that have lived a long life and a free one, out in the air scratching about for worms and bugs and filling their crops with grit. And even really old-fashioned butchers seldom have such birds for sale. So this is largely a country pleasure, one that depends on your own old birds or perhaps those of your neighbors as our first batch did.

Most old hens are best for stock, the finest of all of which comes from them, though old guineas make a fine substitute. The cooking must be long and slow, six hours at the least at a moderate heat to get the best out of the bird. We usually then strain the stock, strip the meat off the bones for the dogs, and burn the bones in the kitchen fireplace, for dogs must not eat cooked bones. But we always sample the meat as we pass it to the dogs, for sometimes the bird is old enough, but not yet too old, to yield truly flavorful meat, and that means a chicken potpie. And usually such birds will have been still of laying age, and so we make a stew with the unborn eggs in ever-decreasing size arranged like a necklace around the pot.

Chicken Stew with Unborn Eggs

Cut up an old hen or rooster. Remove the innards, reserve the liver. Stew bone-in at low heat until the meat is tender. The cooking time will depend entirely on the age of the bird, but 3–4 hours is common and sometimes as much as 6. Half an hour before the meat is tender, add carrots, onions, celeriac, and turnips.

Strip the meat off the bones and return it to the pot.

When you removed the innards, you will have found the ovary, which will contain many days' worth of unformed eggs consisting of only the yolks in ever-decreasing size. Add a dozen or so to the stew, arranging them around the pot in descending order of size. Let them cook a few minutes until firm.

Serve immediately.

RADISHES

A friend of ours once experienced an epiphany with radishes. Through accidental connections, she found herself among dinner guests at a fine, high, old white house in Connecticut, belonging to a fine, high, old family. She conjectured that they had either spent the last of the money that had trickled down for generations, or perhaps they simply preferred to eschew ostentation because that was what good people did. Either option seemed to her the elegant choice. The house was in disrepair, the fine ancient damask drapes were tattered shreds, and no old wing or side chair was quite safe to sit in. It was summer, and drinks were on the lawn, served to guests in a scattering of wicker chairs. Hors d'oeuvres (or nibbles, as they were called) were obligatory, and so, as ice cubes tinkled in cut-glass tumblers, a bowl of radishes was passed around, with good chilled butter and some grainy salt. In our friend's eyes, the austerity, simplicity, and elegance of this offering accorded perfectly with the faint chill of the early New England summer and the fine, stiff manners of her hosts. She had never particularly cared for radishes before. It was a conversion, and she has loved them ever since.

How and when we first enjoy a vegetable for itself alone, rather than as something that is good for you and you should clean your plate, remains in the minds of many of us. We can remember our first artichoke, for example, its slow, inevitable unveiling, so like the act of learning the body of another and taking it into oneself. Similar awakenings have occurred with spinach, when the slow fingers of a patient cook firmly hold the rib, each leaf in one hand, and tear the wings away. Sautéed in butter with perhaps a garlic clove, the result is the succulent essence of green without any strings attached. There is simply nothing like a potato new dug from the ground, the crunch when it is sliced raw and the savor when it is cooked and eaten. No other potato, however carefully homegrown, stored in sand or peat, can quite match that musical sound of slicing or that taste. And so it is with radishes. Fresh pulled, ice-cold, passed around with chilled butter and Maldon salt, they are themselves. Just exactly what a radish should be.

Radishes and butter have a surprising connection. The diarist Samuel Pepys, Irma Rombauer tells us in *Joy of Cooking*, enjoyed them at the table of William Penn. But what radishes might they have been? Not probably Cherry Belles or long White Icicles, both sturdy reliables for their satisfying crunch in early summer. Served with butter, if you think of butter, as our colonial ancestors did, as something like cheese. Probably the radishes eaten by Pepys at Penn's table were more substantial turniplike things, such as Black Spanish or even something like the Japanese daikon. Still, even the crisp raw root we usually think of when we think radish can be cooked, or rather warmed, as in Deborah

Madison's recipe for Braised Red Radishes in *Vegetarian Cooking for Everyone*.

Like many other vegetables, the history of the guileless radish is surprisingly complicated, with many varieties, some yet to be discovered by current-day cooks and gardeners.

The radish arises first in China in ancient times and then spreads westward, to Greece and Rome and all of Europe. It continues to be cultivated even after the fall of the empire and was much prized in medieval gardens for its medicinal qualities—it is rich in vitamin C and so used to treat colds and scurvy. But the radishes grown in the ancient and medieval worlds were not the radishes that we know today. They were long, tapering roots rather like salsify or the Asian semilongs of current use. Little round radishes didn't arise until the late 1500s, first in Holland and then in Italy. Last summer we grew the Philadelphia White Box radish, which traces its ancestry back to the late Renaissance. Cherry Belle, Cherriette, Rover, and so on, however, are all modern selections. And the French breakfast sorts don't appear until the late 1600s.

The other great strain of radishes are the Asian varieties. Some are long and white; daikon is the best example of this sort. Others, largely Chinese, are round, often with pink flesh. The Asian radish typically takes longer to mature, sometimes spending two months in the ground before harvest. These sorts store well in a crock of damp sand stood in a cool place.

Rather like Asian radishes, at least in piquancy and ease of storage, Black Spanish is visually striking, coal black about the size of a turnip with ice-white flesh. We have eaten it in April from an October harvest, its crispness and sharp flavor undiminished by long storage. The Germans eat it with beer. So do we.

Radishes were once served in America with virtually every meal, breakfast included. At North Hill they often accompany our own bacon and our own eggs on the morning table. Freshly harvested radishes are vastly finer even than those bought at farmers' markets. Dipped in Maldon salt they are one of the joys of rural life.

RHUBARB

Rhubarb, though it is of course a herbaceous perennial, is the year's first fruit. And like all the first things that come after winter—green garlic and wild salads and radishes or, for that matter, witch hazels and snowdrops—we prize it as much for its earliness as for its beauty. Its uses on the table give great value to what would be wonderful to see in any case. For by April our apples and pears are wizened, our citrus is all harvested, and the fruit offered in the market seems either insipid or so suspiciously laden with chemicals that it is the opposite of what fruit should be, good and healthful.

Something fresh is wanted, and something we have not tasted in a year. We also want our own rhubarb, harvested from plants that have grown for more than twenty years in our garden.

It is easy to forget how rich in culinary things our time is.

The past five hundred years have piled our tables high with produce unknown to our ancestors, or to the Romans, great gourmets and cooks, who would have marveled at the abundance and variety of our foods. Beans, potatoes, corn, squash, tomatoes, peppers, and eggplants are all products of the New World. By contrast, most of the leafy vegetables we eat are Old World plants cultivated by the Romans. All our familiar fruits—apples, pears, plums, quinces, grapes, figs, lemons, and blackberries—are also Old World plants, having been cultivated for millennia. Rhubarb, too, has long been grown in European gardens, but as a physic plant, not for culinary purposes, as the name of one species, *Rheum officinale*, indicates, the *officina* being the medical dispensary of medieval monasteries. Bitter-tasting tinctures of its leaves and roots, and of those also of *Rheum palmatum*, a related species, have been used in Chinese medicine for over three thousand years, and in England were the laxative of choice well into the nineteenth century. Now, both *R. officinale*, with its vast four-foot-wide lettuce-green leaves, and *R. palmatum*, with equally large, intricately cut leaves—unusually handsome in the purple-leaved variety, *atropurpureum*—are used as striking accents in the perennial and shrubbery borders.

The well-established reputation of rhubarb as a medicinal drug, however, stood in the way of its acceptance as a desirable table "fruit." (Imagine, for example, trying to market an ice cream flavored with Milk of Magnesia.) What eventually altered attitudes was the introduction of a new species in the early nineteenth century from Siberia, *Rheum undulatum*, which, when crossed with the older medicinal species, produced plants that for the most part were much more palatable, especially when mixed liberally with sugar. Culinary rhubarb was first introduced to the Covent Garden market in London in 1808, but only three bundles sold. Shoppers who nibbled on a stalk found them unpleasantly sour, reminiscent of something "medicinal." Thirty years later, rhubarb had become a national obsession with the English, and by century's end there were at least thirty known cultivars, representing complex crosses and backcrosses of species to the extent that all cultivated rhubarb goes under the botanical name *Rheum x cultorum*, and only DNA research can untangle the genetic descent of any plant cultivated today.

Many Victorian rhubarbs were chosen more for their enormous size than the fineness of their flavor. The names themselves are noteworthy, emphasizing size, color, earliness of sprouting, and—most tellingly—connections with the British royal family, which took rhubarb up with a passion, thus encouraging its general popularity. So early varieties were named Buck's Early Red, Early Scarlet, Early Pontic, Scarlet Nonpareil, Radford's Scarlet, Goliath, and Victoria, Prince Albert, Monarch, Prince of Wales, and Princess Royal. Most of these have fallen out of fashion, at least in America, though Kent Whealy's *Fruit, Berry and Nut Inventory* lists thirteen varieties available in America. Of the Victorian sorts, only Victoria itself has remained popular in America today. America followed Britain in enthusiasm for this new "fruit," but even in the twentieth century Continental Europe was slow to embrace it. It is to this day little grown in France, though its popularity has increased in Germany, Poland, and Russia.

Part of the popularity of rhubarb in Britain and to a lesser degree in America was the ease with which it could be forced. Before the rise of widespread commercial agriculture and long-haul transport, estates prided themselves on their self-sufficiency and vied with one another to bring to the table fruits and vegetables ever earlier in the season and even out of season. Rhubarb proved remarkably easy to force, either by using fresh "hot" animal manures to warm the outdoor beds or, better, by lifting the roots and taking them into heated indoor space. Rhubarb roots could even be induced to grow packed in wooden boxes and set beside a wood-burning kitchen stove. So the plant, which is harvestable here in late April or very early May, came to be prized as a compote on the Christmas table.

Rhubarb is a handsome plant, with two-foot-wide, hairy, puckered, dark green leaves arranged in a graceful mound on stems three feet tall. In midsummer they are crowned by shafts of creamy bloom as tall as eight feet, and then by beautiful thickly clustered seed heads made up of thousands of tiny yellow-green papery wafers centered by a reddish-brown seed. Gardening books often insist that these inflorescences be removed, so as not to weaken the roots. But many gardeners admire the flowers so much that they take the chance and, really, it does not seem to cause any harm, if the plants are well tended. At Great Dixter, for example, they are never robbed of their bloom and have been in abundant continuous production since the bed was established by Christopher Lloyd's parents in 1911.

In fact, for many years we grew culinary rhubarb as an ornamental plant in our rhododendron garden, along with its cousins, *R. palmatum* and *R. officinale*. It formed a fine bold contrast to the *Epimediums* and gingers and woodland grasses that grow there between the rhododendrons, but as that garden grew shadier, it began to suffer and weaken, to the extent that no leaves were harvestable, and the plant itself was shrinking each year. When we finally rescued it, there were not more than a dozen wizened divisions that showed growing eyes. We could of course have acquired fresh new roots easily, either from mail-order catalogs or local nurseries, and then we would know what rhubarb variety we are growing; as it is, after twenty or more years, we haven't a clue. But we are sentimental about our plants, and certainly about the reuse of one we almost let slip into extinction by inattention. So we dug our frail divisions and vowed to do better by them.

Actually, it took only one growing season to return them to

harvestable vigor. Rhubarb is a very fast-growing plant, given the one thing it demands, which is the best that you can give it. A pit must be dug at least eighteen inches deep, preferably in autumn, and filled with all the rich stuff you have—partly decomposed compost, animal manures, leaves and grass clippings— to rot over winter. In very early spring, scatter a handful of 5-10-10 for each plant over the bottom of the pit and then cover with six inches of plain soil. The crowns of rhubarb can be established as close as two feet from one another, but four feet is better. The soil of the bed must never be allowed to dry out, and it should be mulched heavily in autumn, the mulch pulled away from the crowns for early harvest but left around the plants all summer. An additional dressing of 5-10-10 should be applied as the shoots appear, taking care not to get any of the fertilizer in the living tip, which will burn it. Harvest may begin as soon as the first leaves are big enough for use, and can continue—in cool weather—well into early July.

Though rhubarb can be stewed or made into conserves and jams, and many people like it that way, for us there is only one rhubarb recipe. That is rhubarb custard pie, a dish first served us by Tasha Tudor during the long years we worked for her. We knew the recipe was of Shaker origin, but in the days before the Internet it proved surprisingly elusive. Finally we found it in a cookbook by Ron Johnson, who had a double identity as both a great scholar of American cooking and a significant poet. Johnson died in 1998, but strangely, one of us had worked with him as a retail clerk in a Japanese pottery store he managed in San Francisco in 1968. As he says in his preface to *The American Table*, "A lot of the recipes in this book are worn smooth as river pebbles . . ." So we have made alterations and adaptations to Johnson's recipe, largely to accommodate the two-and-a-half-inch-deep pie plate we favor, and because we like a cinnamony sort of pie. Here is our version.

Rhubarb Custard Pie

   4 tablespoons butter

   2¼ c. granulated sugar

   4 tablespoons flour

   Nutmeg, freshly grated

   4 eggs

   5–6 stalks rhubarb

   Cinnamon, granulated sugar, and butter

First prepare a batch of good flaky American piecrust. For both amateurs and experienced pie makers alike, we have found Irma Rombauer's flour-paste method in *Joy of Cooking* to be foolproof. Set the dough aside. Then melt 4 tablespoons of butter and put aside. Measure 2¼ cups of granulated sugar into a bowl and whisk in 4 tablespoons of flour. Add a generous grating of fresh nutmeg, 4 fresh eggs, and the melted butter. Whisk this mixture until smooth and buttery.

Grease a deep pie dish with butter. Divide the piecrust in two, and roll out one half on a generously floured surface. Using the blade of a long, thin knife, free one half of the piecrust by sliding the knife between the surface and the dough. Fold that half over gently, and free the other half in the same way. Lift the piecrust gently over the pie plate, aligning the center crease down its middle, and unfold it to cover the plate. Press down lightly to mold the crust to the plate.

Cut the rhubarb with kitchen shears into ½-inch pieces until they loosely fill the pie plate. (Shears work better than a knife because they cut cleanly through the threads of the stalks.) If the stalks are very wide, slit them in half with a sharp knife before snipping them. You will need five or six stalks, depending on their size, but it is much better to have too much than too little. When the plate is full, pour in the egg custard mix. Roll out the top crust and cut it into ½-inch strips. Lay these strips over the pie, first in one direction and then in the opposite, to form a lattice. (Aretha Franklin has taught us that it is not necessary to do the weaving business with a lattice crust. The pie will come out pretty anyway.) Press the crust down lightly and crimp the edges. Dust the top first with cinnamon, then with granulated sugar, and dot with butter.

Slide the pie into a preheated 450° oven, and bake for 10 minutes to set the dough. Then reduce the oven to 350° and bake until the crust is brown and the filling is bubbly, about 40 minutes.

Serve the pie warm, with ice cream or whipped cream if you wish.

We make this pie about five or six times from May to very early July, and of course we serve it to guests at early summer lunches. Our summer climate provides the cool nights that rhubarb relishes, and so we could perhaps continue cutting throughout July and even well into August. But by mid-July other ripe fruits are upon us, and we give our rhubarb a rest, glorying only in its tall, stately plumes of flower and its wonderful seed heads.

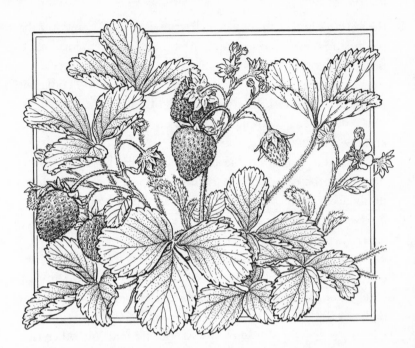

STRAWBERRIES

Our sweetest memory, literally, is of our first June in Vermont. We did not come here by accident. To live in Vermont, the most rural, least populated of the New England states, was a considered decision made for many reasons. They were in part political. Vermont in the early '70s was already the most progressive state in the Union. But more important, we came for the land. With its small tree-clad mountains, its narrow valleys abundant with flowing streams, its charming villages, for two boys who wanted a rural life there was no place finer. And Vermont, from the first, filled our lap with its charms. We moved out of Boston in August. The summer was ending but we caught its last two warm weeks. And then came autumn in all its orange splendor. The winter, then, with deep snow upon the ground for months. The blushing spring followed, flowers everywhere, lilacs, quince, apples, and finally, in May, the heartbreaking greening of the forest, at first the palest green, a color so tender we would both just sit and stare at what we had not seen before. And then it was June. One June weekend Joe's father came to visit. He had, as a boy, lived for a time on a farm in Pennsylvania and he always kept a deep fondness for country things. It was he who suggested early one Sunday morning that we go out to the fields and look for wild strawberries. Neither of us had ever done this, but he had many times as a boy. Baskets in hand, we began wandering the fields. Strawberries were everywhere. Not, of course, at all like those one bought in markets. These wild things were tiny, not larger than a fingertip. So small were they that hours passed before our baskets were full. That night we had them with a dusting of sugar and fresh cream from a neighboring farm.

When we made our garden, strawberries were among the first we planted. We made four beds fifteen feet long and three feet wide. We planted bare root plants ordered from Miller's, the celebrated fruit nursery in the Finger Lakes region of New York. We mulched them with straw to keep the roots cool and moist and also to keep dirt from soiling the fruit when we got fruit, which would, this first year, not be until late summer. And this first year we would get only a few from the one everbearing, Tristar, which we planted. The three other varieties were all once-fruiting sorts bearing fruit for three weeks or so in late June and July. And none of those we planted bore particularly early, for as we heard from many old farmers, the later the berry, the sweeter. We remember that Sparkle was one of these varieties and its fruit was indeed fine. But with Sparkle, only the first picking was completely satisfying. Thereafter, the berries, though still full of flavor, grew smaller and the plants bore less abundantly. Still, we stayed with it until about twenty years ago when we discovered Jewel. This plant has a fine rich strawberry flavor, bears very heavily and consistently for three weeks, and is resistant to most diseases. If we had to name a favorite variety, Jewel would be it. It is not to be confused with the California berries we find in markets always but especially in May and June, which though they appear delectable are usually merely sweet but bland with flavor. Jewel, on the other hand, is the essence of strawberry.

With all strawberries, even everbearers until perhaps mid-August, newly established plants should have all their blossoms picked off. Though painful to do, the rewards the following year are richly abundant flavorful fruit.

But it would be false to imply that we had no strawberries that first year. We did have wildlings and a selection of our wild strawberry, *fraises des bois*. White Flower Farm in Litchfield, Connecticut, a nursery that prides itself on offerings both unusual and elegant, had just listed *fraises des bois* or Alpine strawberries. They were in fact first discovered in the Alps, near Grenoble. And though simply a variant on our native strawberry, they have two very desirable characteristics. The plants are large, four or five inches tall and perhaps three inches across. The fruit also is a bit larger than wildlings. But this selection's great gift to the gardener is that it bears from June to September. In the early nineteenth century, many varieties were named, but they seem little different one from the other. Except for one characteristic that some possess: Their fruit is white or pale yellow when ripe. In fragrance or taste they are like their red cousins, but birds find them unappealing and so they need not be netted.

Alpine strawberries are effective in the ornamental garden, especially for edging. Where the pocketbook is an issue, they make a good stand-in for boxwood lining a bed or path.

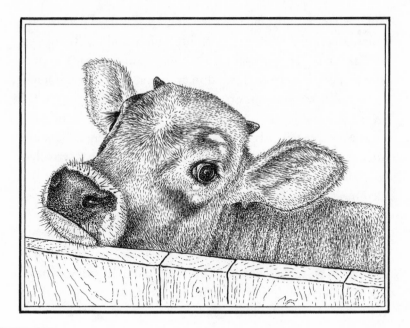

VEAL CALF

For many years—twenty-one, in fact—we had a snow-white cow named Livia. She was part of a small Scots Highlands herd we have kept here almost since the beginning of the garden. There have never been more than six or seven, and for many years she was the Boss Cow. People generally think of bulls as very dominant animals, but cow herds are in fact matriarchal societies, and the oldest, strongest female makes all the essential decisions. Livia came to us as a sleek, handsome white heifer, and the year after her arrival she bore a beautiful little white bull calf. Shortly thereafter she assumed her role as Supreme Ruler, but she never succeeded in raising another calf.

Livia experienced a condition common among beef cows, of teats so enlarged that the infant animal could not successfully get its mouth around them to nurse. The second infant she bore tried valiantly and failed, weakening by the day. We had recourse to every device we could think of, including attempting to milk Livia, though as anyone familiar with beef cows knows, they do not countenance that familiarity, and a good kick is likely to be one's punishment. So we tried a giant milk bottle filled with supermarket milk and held just under the little animal's nose. Somehow, we were no substitute for Mother, and finally, after becoming more and more frail, he died. That was actually a relief, for we woke each morning anxious for his life, and struggled most of the day to preserve it. We buried him with a sense of peace, both for him and for us.

And a resolution. From then on, both Livia and we would be spared, she from a painfully engorged udder and the sense of not being able to tend her child, and we from the agony of watching a small life pining away by inches. We decided to steal future calves the moment they were born—if we could get there—and become foster mothers, raising them ourselves.

It is not an easy thing to steal a calf away from its mother. Timing is crucial. After the calf drops, the cow is dazed and spends some time consuming the afterbirth, which stimulates the first flow of milk, the colostrum, which is both very rich and also triggers the calf's immune system. (Indeed, recognizing this fact, from the medieval period well into the early nineteenth century, wise women brought puddings made from colostrum to invalids and new mothers.) Without that first rich suck, the calf will be prone to a host of ills and chills, and will never grow up to be a healthy animal. Also, calves are generally born at a very difficult time, in the snows of early April, when they shiver pitifully without the warming sustenance of a mother's milk.

But once the cow has turned her attention to the calf, and licked it, whether it can nurse or not, she becomes bonded to it and is fiercely defensive. In the case of Scots Highlands, that defense consists primarily of very long horns, which the mother can wield with the precision of an Olympic fencer. She can also kick. So one has only a very brief window for taking the calf, and one must hope one is awake and not befogged by last night's Burgundy, and that the calf has been dropped close to the fence. A deep breath is required. And also a cane, something that looks as if it would aid a person of uncertain steps in negotiating tricky sidewalks but in fact is to be bought at any farm supply store and is meant to hook the calf by its leg and pull it under the fence. Once this is achieved, the rest is comparatively easy. Or at least not dangerous. You simply have to cradle a bloody, slimy bundle weighing perhaps seventy pounds and run like hell. Once in a safe, dry stall full of fresh bedding hay, you dry off the calf with old towels, make it feel like life is a good thing, and wait three or four hours—maybe more—until it is ready to suck up its first meal. For it will have some residual food in its tummy from its mother's womb, and in any case, it is very confusing to be born.

Then comes the real challenge, and it is of three sorts. First, one must have a good supply of colostrum on hand. Half a milking bottle will be enough, but though baby calf bottles look exactly like baby bottles, calf bottles hold two quarts. Fortunately, colostrum does not lose its therapeutic values when frozen, and so, being country people, we can generally lay in a supply when we see the cow swell and approach birth. We call Mrs. Wheeler, who runs a dairy farm in nearby Wilmington, and she puts some by for us from cows in her herd that have recently given birth. Equipped with this, we are ready for the second challenge.

Which is convincing the little animal that nursing is a good idea. It takes patience, and anyone who has watched an infant calf try to decide where the good things are will understand. It is all very confusing and involves a good bit of poking and prying into the wrong places. For us, the easiest way is to put the calf firmly between our legs and force the nipple down its throat. There will be false starts, but eventually the right idea comes into its dim little head, and it sucks peacefully. Not too much at first, because a calf will suck itself to death if allowed to. A cow's udder regulates the flow according to what is appropriate, and indeed, a calf will butt an udder—or even a bottle or pail—in an attempt to stimulate more milk. (For foster mothers, such as us, this can be extremely irritating, when the pail of milk is thrown back into our faces.) Occasionally, one does overdo it, and then scours result, a form of flux that can dehydrate the calf and result even in death. Then the remedy is to substitute an electrolyte solution for the milk—Bounce Back is the descriptive name—until the calf becomes stable again and real milk can be fed. Any mother knows this.

As the calf grows larger, it is important to teach it to drink out of a bucket on its own, for there is a limit to the number of half-gallon-size baby bottles you can carry to the stall, and a calf nearing term may drink as many as five or six quarts three times a day. That's the third challenge, for a calf—or, we suppose, any baby: There is something fundamentally satisfying about sucking at a nipple. It is a difficult habit to change. Country people have various methods. Some submerge the rubber nipple into the bucket and tilt the calf's head toward it. Others use their finger, dipped in milk and held to the calf's mouth, gently lowering it into the milk. And some—the impatient—simply plunge the calf's head into the bucket, and say, "Drink, damn it! You're going to have to sooner or later!" We prefer the submerged nipple method. It seems gentler, somehow.

But what is real milk? We have been through many answers to this question. In the beginning, in our first zeal, we got five-gallon plastic pails of raw milk from a local farmer, and that worked well until a full five gallons tipped over onto our car floor, and then, while going for another, something like a hurricane turned the light green and dumped trees onto the road just in front of us. For a time, we compromised our fundamental principles by substituting powdered milk, which was certainly convenient (if expensive) but lacked essential fats and nutrients. Now we have gone with organic whole milk, which we buy in gallon cartons at the supermarket and to which we add beaten-up duck eggs, a sort of milk shake for the calf. It is a very French sort of thing to do. The eggs increase the albumen in the veal, which contributes that succulence to veal that is why one treasures it in the kitchen. (Besides, if you are not baking a cake, what do you do with duck eggs?)

We have raised a veal calf every year for almost thirty years, and we have not done it to save poor Livia or to return a healthy calf to the herd (though we have in fact done this, from time to time). We have raised them for their meat. Elsewhere in this book, we make an argument for the wisdom of this. We can only restate here that if one is going to eat the flesh of animals, one had better be sure that they are humanely treated, bedded on fresh sweet-smelling straw, carefully tended during their lives, and treasured to the end. We could not eat anything, actually, if we were not sure we had taken that sort of care.

Wiener Schnitzel

This is our son Fotios's favorite recipe, prepared for him on every visit he makes to North Hill. It is extraordinarily simple, but like all simple foods everything depends on the quality of the ingredients. Our ingredients are our own veal scallops, our own eggs, and bread crumbs from the Silver Moon Bakery in New York, the best in Manhattan. And olive oil from our son's own trees in the Mani.

Pound the scallops almost to paper thin between two pieces of plastic wrap. Dip them in egg and then in bread crumbs, and fry them ever so briefly in olive oil. When they are bronzed and crisp, take them from the pan and set them on paper towels so some of the grease drains away. When you have done the batch, take them to the table and dress them with citrus, lemon or lime, and (Maldon) salt, if desired. Our citrus comes from our own greenhouse.

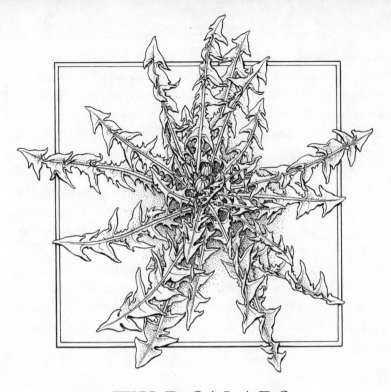

WILD SALADS

In spring, the gardens of our friends, particularly when they are not very well weeded, are rich in possibilities. So are the edges of the rural woods, or any country roadside or damp ditch not contaminated by road salts, and any pasture not freshly manured. For in all these places there are delicious salads to gather. We frequently find ourselves, particularly in gardens, saying, "You know, you could *eat* that." We are almost always met with unbelieving stares, or worse, that sort of indulgent smile that conveys that one has lapsed again and is not quite nailed down tight. Once a friend followed our suggestion and made a wild salad, only to be met with her granddaughter's wail, "Grandma! These are weeds!" And a kind friend once took over the washing of the salad, one of the few kitchen tasks we are willing to delegate, and remarked, "That lettuce was awfully full of weeds, but I picked them all out."

The truth is that though legions of Italian and Greek women and children fan out over the rural countryside each spring and into the olive groves gathering enormous heaps of greens, *erba rifatta* in Italy and *horta* in Greece, most Americans consider anything not grown in the pristine purity of a vegetable garden, on purpose, or worse, bought at the supermarket, somehow very suspect. "Can't you get poisoned?" is too often the response we get when we suggest wild greens of any sort. This suspicion ignores the reality that one is far more likely to contract *E. coli* from a head of Romaine lettuce grown in California, unsanitarily packed in bacteria-friendly plastic bags, shipped for two days across country to lie in a humid, mist-bathed supermarket bin for two or three days more. The press is full of bad things that have happened to people who have eaten some of that stuff, and yet the prejudice against wild-harvested greens continues.

But all over America, in rural areas and even untilled fields at the edges of large towns, there are people who impatiently wait for spring. Mostly they are of three sorts: genuine country dwellers whose parents and grandparents have searched the fields, perhaps even from colonial times, for the first edible greens; immigrants to America, who, even after the second or third generation here, retain a memory of the good things that can be gathered wild; and people like us, who pay attention to culinary habits and traditions and tastes that stretch far back, even to the ancient Celts who gathered wild cabbage on the cliffs of Dover.

There is something deeply satisfying about gathering wild greens—greater even than growing vegetables, and certainly different from the routine trip to the supermarket to buy something for dinner. Glorious spring days in which one has nothing to do but work in the garden, and can shoulder one's hoe and head off with a bag of seeds and a basket for an early harvest of radishes before one's mood is the least bit tarnished by answering a soliciting phone call or paying the electricity bill, such days are fine. But finer still—or maybe just finer in a different way—is another glorious spring day in which one heads out to search for the first crowns of dandelion, the first daylily shoots, the first newly sprouted stems of mint in roadside ditches. It is a brisk walk in the country, a mission with a purpose, and a chance to enjoy the beauty of the spring without even the sense of all the chores in the garden that should have been done before or must be done now.

The trick for a very good wild salad is to accumulate the largest number of different greens one possibly can, for though a wild salad will be greater than the sum of its parts, each individual leaf will contribute its own qualities, of bitter or sour, sharp or bland or spicy. But probably the foundation of all wild spring salads is dandelions, naturalized descendants of *Taraxacum officinale*, all descendants of plants brought by the early colonists to America as a cooking green and now naturalized in fields and along roadsides throughout most of North America. It is a very hardy plant, with a long yellow taproot and a rosette of dark, toothed green leaves forming a ground-hugging rosette in spring and a taller upright plant as it matures. Though it is the bane of many homeowners who crave weed-free lawns and exterminate it with Weed 'n Feed, we treasure every one, furnishing our salad bowl and weeding our lawn all at once. But though the button buds at the center of a young rosette are also delicious, harvesting ceases when the first ragged-petaled yellow flower opens, for then the greens will be too tough and bitter for salad.

There is an art to harvesting dandelions that saves much time in the kitchen. When you locate a fat rosette, gather its leaves together in one hand, and with the other probe with an old kitchen knife below it and sever the crown about a half inch below ground level. You can then hold the green leaves in one hand and comb down last year's brown ones and any clinging debris with the other, severing the leaves just above the point where they emerge from the crown. That is a great deal easier than picking them clean in the kitchen.

A second staple to spring salad is wild mustard, actually two species, *Barbarea vulgaris* and *B. verna*, both called St. Barbara's weed because traditionally they were the only green thing available on the Feast of St. Barbara, which falls on December 4. Both plants bear many common names—St. Barbara's weed, winter cress, upland cress, land cress, yellow rocket, Belle Isle cress and, most tellingly, scurvy grass, indicating, as a plethora of common names always does, a very long history in gardens. Though once a commonly cultivated garden plant, it now mostly shows up as a biennial weed in cultivated fields, where in spring it can turn bare earth into a sheet of gold. It is there for the gathering, and in early spring its leaves possess a pleasing sharp cress taste. Later, as it matures, it is excellent cooked in the Italian fashion, barely wilted with plenty of garlic fried in olive oil. The beautiful daffodil yellow flowers may also be added to salads for color, though when adding any flower to salads, whether cultivated nasturtiums or daylilies or violets, sprinkle them over the top after the salad is dressed, lest they become draggled and dirty looking from the dressing.

Among bland greens to go with these sharp and bitter tastes, we treasure both young violet leaves and flowers. We pick from plants of *Viola sororia*, the native field or Confederate Violet, so-called from the resemblance of its violet-gray flowers to the sadly faded uniforms of Confederate soldiers, though with fair frequency, darker bluish flowers will appear among them, proof that all is long since resolved. We take the youngest leaves, which offer a nice dark green contrast and a slightly leathery texture, and the flowers, held off separately to sprinkle over at the end. Our fields are full of wild violets, but so are the flower beds, for whoever called violets "shy" had no experience with their promiscuous ways.

There is no place in rural New England where patches of daylilies are not common along the roadside. Mostly they are *Hemerocallis fulva*, the tawny daylily introduced from Europe as an ornamental garden plant but then widely naturalized to the extent that it has earned the common name ditch daylily and has been listed by the USDA as an invasive species. Occasionally one will also see a patch of *H. fulva* "Kwanzo," though they must be the result of some gardener's having too much, and therefore "throwing them in the ditch." Both provide edible shoots in early spring, readily available since ditches warm up first. The shoots have a rich nutlike flavor, and if the greening tops have become tough, they may be snipped away, leaving only the ivory trough-shaped leaves.

For a note of bitter, one can almost always find new shoots of chicory (*Chicorium intybus*) in early spring along any roadside bordering a field. Of course, one must know one's roadside, for if it has been salted in winter snowstorms, or worse, treated with herbicides, that is not the place to gather a salubrious salad of early spring greens. Chicory is also an escaped garden plant, so long established as to be considered an American native wild-flower, and still called succory by many rural Americans. Its limpid blue flowers can be seen almost anywhere in late July and August, and they, too, add a pretty note to summer salads or garnishes to cold meats.

Two lowly plants are essential to wild spring salads. One is chickweed, *Stellaria media*, which, for all the innocence of its name, can choke a dampish vegetable plot in no time at all. So much the better, we feel, though most of it goes to the chickens, who relish it. We always clip away the tips, possibly with the minute and lovely tiny white flowers that give it both its Latin and English name, star weed, to toss into the salad bowl. *Stellaria* is actually grown in England and Europe as a salad crop, and where it is not in our way, we leave its watery clumps of growth, taking off only the tops and hoping for a subsequent harvest.

The taste of the leaves and stems is fresh, watery, and mild, almost like the very best lettuces.

The other lowly weed we value is purslane (*Portulaca olericea*), which old Vermonters hereabout still call pusley. We are told by Irma Rombauer in her *Joy of Cooking* that it was Gandhi's favorite vegetable, and in fact good large-leaved forms of it have been offered, usually golden, to grow in the vegetable garden as greens for cooking. We prefer the wild, green form, which sprouts plentifully as a weed on tilled ground, crabbing along the surface of the soil. Only the succulent tips should be taken and if the plants are not in rows one wants to sow, they might as well be left for future harvests. Otherwise, the pigs love them.

Mint is the final essential ingredient of our vernal mixed salads. Because of its rampant ways we do not grow mint in our own garden, though we have grown it elsewhere, in frostproof terra-cotta chimney tiles sunk into the earth. But mint is an escape artist, and forms of it, peppermint or spearmint, crinkled or smooth, have escaped over the many years that gardens have been cultivated in Vermont, and several forms are apparent in ditches hereabouts, and even a fine crinkled form in our own stream. We search for them and, in the spring, we pinch out just the top first whorl of leaves, which are mild, tender, and gently minty. We could establish a patch or two, according to the containment methods we know, but it is more fun to search out the wild plants, though we know that every one of them once had a pedigree in an old vanished garden near here.

Even we are a little conflicted about other wild greens that grow near us. We have plenty of lamb's quarters, an amiable name for pigweed, which has an even finer name in Latin, *Chenopodium bonus-henricus*. (Which good King Henry? we wonder.) It has been eaten for a long while by our neighbors, who harvest it for something liked cooked spinach. And we have tossed its purplish-green leaves into salads when we found them sprouting wild in our well-tended vegetable garden and then extracted them from our plates at the table, as something a little too chewy. It is not good to be too rapid in one's rejection of anything, but it is still important to know what one really wants and enjoys eating.

Our list of wild-growing salads is hardly exhaustive. We'd gather watercress if we could, for though it does not grow native in southern Vermont, we could easily establish stands of it along our stream from hydroponically grown bunches bought from the supermarket. But *Giardia*—so-called beaver fever—exists even in the purest streams, and we are unwilling to take that chance. If we lived where miner's lettuce grew, chiefly in California and the Northwest, we would harvest it with both hands, for its rounded leaves through which a stem pierces with tiny, beautiful white flowers are delicious.

Still, we have a rich harvest here, and as our knowledge grows, our spring salad bowl becomes more varied. We have much to learn, and there are many guides available, starting with Euell Gibbons's *Stalking the Wild Asparagus*, published forty years ago. There are even stylish restaurants in major cities that feature wild greens that are even called "wild greens," though some of their salads are composed of garden-grown species of native or naturalized plants.

Though, like the Romans, we might prefer wild-gathered asparagus to anything grown in a garden plot. For we share the thrill that Diana Kennedy, the great scholar of Mexican cooking, once experienced when she found epazote naturalized in Central Park. A native of Mexico and Guatemala and an essential ingredient of much Mexican and Central American cooking, epazote is *Chenopodium ambrosioides*, a close relative of Good King Henry, though far more pungent. There it was, mysteriously, free for the gathering.

BEANS

For some years when the Great Pea Harvest was finished, the garden entered a quiet season. There was still plenty to eat, of course, salads and carrots and beets and beans, but the next great celebration waited on the ripening of tomatoes and, even more, on the corn harvest. This should not have been. We grew what we thought were good American bean varieties, largely bush type, Burpee's Tenderpick and Purple Queen, Vermont Bean Seed's Provider, Veseys' Maxibel, Pine Trees Bountiful. And we grew pole beans as well, especially Kentucky Wonder, generally thought the best of all. Yet to us they seemed all to possess a bland sameness, never ascending to the status of something you really look forward to eating. Well, we thought, beans just aren't as good as peas.

Some years later, in Rome, we stumbled upon a small shop that sold gardening things—pots and fertilizer and seeds. The seeds were packaged in great large packs with brilliant photographs on their covers. Their names were all in Italian so we knew not what we were buying. But buy we did, all manner of things, chicory and lettuce and artichokes and, more than anything else, beans. The combination of name and photograph made them irresistible. Fagiolo Rampicante and Meraviglia di Venezia, for example, great vigorous climbing beans with broad flat yellow pods of extraordinary flavor. And Fagioli Rampicante Supermarconi, also vigorously climbing and equally flavorful if more green than yellow.

A dish of pasta con fagioli eaten in an outdoor café with family caused us to seek out shelling beans. We are particularly fond of Borlotto Lamon, a climbing bean with beautiful red-and-white mottled shells with small brown-speckled beans, considered the finest of all the shelling beans. We usually grow six or eight different varieties of pole bean, trained up on an eight-foot arch of bamboo that covers the center part of the central path. It is high enough that one can walk under it, always a pleasure in any garden.

Of course we grow bush beans, too, because they mature earlier and also because they occupy much less space. Like pole beans, they come in a great variety of forms. Slender Green Baby Bianca matures as early as fifty-five days whereas most pole beans take seventy days at least to reach picking size. Brittle Wax is golden yellow, slender, also early, but it bears all its crop at once so you must sow small numbers every ten days or so for a longer harvest. Marconi is a flat green Roman type, good but not as flavorful as Supermarconi. In fact, none of the bush beans equals the pole beans in flavor whatever advantage they offer in compactness and earliness.

But our fondness for beans bought from Seeds of Italy, the American supplier for Franchi Sementi, should not prejudice you away from the bounty of bean varieties available from American sources. The Seed Savers Exchange lists more than four thousand cultivars for all sorts of beans: green, wax, purple, pole, bush, and everything in between. These are all genetically the same species, *Phaseolus vulgaris*, and all forms readily cross with each other. Hence there are probably more bean varieties than any other vegetable we eat. There is a Dutch variety named Dragon Langerie, whose pods are mottled purple and cream. The flavor is called remarkably good by Pinetree Garden Seeds in Maine, which sells it. It is a bush bean so we are sure we can find a place for it.

But cultivars of the North American *Phaseolus vulgaris* are not the only legume we consume. Long before beans were discovered in the New World, Europeans ate fava beans or broad beans. A recipe for fava called Fabaciae Virides et Baianae appears in the Roman cookbook by Apicius. But the ancients ate a small podded bean whereas the modern fava dates from only about the year A.D. 800 and originated in Spain. It was originally dried and ground for flour; it is only in modern times that the bean has been harvested in its green state. The best Italian variety for northern gardens is Cascicum, which ripens in seventy-five to eighty days. This is important, for heat carries favas off so they must be early maturing. Luckily, they are largely impervious to cold and so can be sown with our earliest crops, peas and radishes and lettuce. For many years we let ours grow any which way, and as they tend to be tall, they would flop all over the ground and into the paths, making picking rather a chore. Last year, however, we saw a beautiful illustration in a British magazine of favas grown through a cat's cradle of twine and we mean to copy the effect ourselves this season. In our climate, the harvest is brief, not more than two weeks before the heat takes them off, but like so much in the garden—cherries and magnolias and many alpines—their very brevity makes them the more treasured.

There are two other beans we cherish, both of which are

relatively new to us. We have long enjoyed Japanese food and certainly enjoyed edamame. But only when Johnny's Selected Seeds began to offer a form called Butter Bean did we attempt it in our own garden. It is tremendously prolific but produces all its crop at once. So we sow it at ten-day intervals for a month or so, for one serving would hardly sate our pleasure in it. You only briefly boil it and dress it with copious amounts of salt; then you drag the pod through your teeth, extracting the bean and of course the salt, which is half the delight of eating them.

The last bean on our long list is the Indian Long Bean. We first encountered them at the Indian markets in Jackson Heights, Queens, and then found that Territorial Seed offered a wonderful variety called Red Noodle. Though they are often called Yard Long Beans, in fact they are about eighteen inches in length and this variety Territorial describes as garnet colored, which is precisely accurate. But they require heat to set fruit, and so in Vermont the only place suitable for them is in the torrid temperatures reached in the lower greenhouse in midsummer. Grown in an enormous pot in the very center, they are so strikingly beautiful it is often hard to pick them. But growing vegetables for their beauty alone is a valid endeavor, and keeping that in mind is the royal road to a vegetable garden one really wants to visit.

Fagioli a Corallo
(Broad Beans or Long Beans)

2 pounds Romano beans, washed and trimmed
3 or 4 garlic cloves
½ cup extra-virgin olive oil
1 or 2 spicy peppers or dried red crushed peppers or
    cayenne
Sea salt

2 cups basil

1 pint ripe grape or cherry or ripe red tomatoes

Place all the ingredients in a large skillet over high heat, covered. Bring to a happy fry and reduce the heat to low. Keep on stirring and cooking, covered, until the beans are very tender, 40 minutes at least.

Taste for seasoning.

SERVES 4

From the kitchen of Beatrice Tosti di Valminuta

BLUEBERRIES

The farm had always been here. Over the river. It grew blueberries. One could buy them by the quart or pick one's own from July to October. The field was vast, perhaps fifty acres, and the bushes were grand, six feet tall and five feet wide, early ones and late ones. But then it died. People still bought blueberries, but now from Hannaford on Putney Road. They did not bother to drive to Keene. And the markets bought from New Jersey, where they could get a whole truckload at once. The economy of local agriculture was dying. A sadness—but for North Hill a gift. We bought eight of the great old bushes, dug them with effort, and brought them home. In an instant the back wall of the vegetable garden was framed, beautiful blueberries in a line. Blueberries have every virtue. They are handsomely shaped, with dark sinuous twigging and foliage that in autumn turns a brilliant red.

In summer they are beset with birds. We could net them, but we have so much we do not need to deny fruit to our birds. Blue jays are the busiest, beautiful blue birds, common but still a gift. Sometimes we stand and watch them, families as they feast. How blessed we are to live in company with so many creatures. In the great net of life we have only to be awake.

So what do we do with blueberries? We eat them simply, with cream, always cream, and a very little sugar. And in pies. Not hard if one knows how to make pies. This is a great American art; no one else knows how to make pies. But we Americans do and it is what we offer to our Asian and European friends, something unique and fine and American.

Just simple aesthetics. Blueberries are elegant and we value them in the garden and on the table. They partner well with azaleas and rhododendrons, needing only filtered light. Those we grow in the garden bear less heavily than those we grow in the vegetable garden. But ours is a large and abundant garden so we can afford a little profligacy just for beauty.

Blueberries are two species, one tall and substantial, the other low and spreading. Each makes delicious fruit. That of the tall one, *Vaccinium corymbosum*, is larger than that of the ground-hugging *Vaccinium angustifolium*. Both are handsome in themselves, not just in what they produce. We use them throughout the garden, particularly in the woodland, where they bear in shady places. When one is a lover, one covets and cherishes all of the other, the little oddnesses of the physical self. To be in love is to have that right. And so with plants. Of course they are beautiful in flower or in autumn all orange and scarlet. But in any season, they are beautiful in their bones in the way the wood bends and twists. So we see blueberries. Darkest brown wood, bending and twisting at angles. It is, we think, what marks them out, the way each twig or branch turns and grows sharply to somewhere else. In this they are like only *Ilex verticillata*. In July and August, we often feast on berries pulled from the bushes while standing in the garden. It is an elemental joy, the nearest we can come to Eden, fruit from the tree. Sometimes we meet a friend there, or each other, or Martha, who lives with us for part of each summer, or Fotios, our son, who is with us for many weekends during the summer, or John or Nicole, gardeners here who share with us the garden's bounty. If gardening has a purpose, it is to engender plenitude, a delicious human fantasy that want is banished. And not unlike the other arts—poetry, music, novels—gardening does try to achieve the real thing, the Eden of our imaginations, here and now.

PIE RECOLLECTIONS
Bobbi Angell, October 19, 2010

Wayne baked me a blueberry pie the last time I saw him. Eating homemade pie at North Hill was not unusual—in fact it was one of the pleasures accompanying my work as illustrator of their books, a definite perk I took advantage of whenever offered. When it was citrus season in their greenhouse, and I needed to draw fruits for an essay in *To Eat*, Wayne baked Joe's favorite Key lime pie. A few months later it was cherry pie, simply because Wayne had found a bountiful supply in Union Square weeks before they would have been ripe in Vermont. He let us know he had pitted each cherry by hand; there was no other way. The pecan pie was because Wayne thought I was too thin—I was to take home the leftovers and eat it with fresh whipped cream. I believe he even lent me the proper copper bowl to beat the cream.

But the blueberry pie was more special. I had considered drawing one when I was ready to illustrate the blueberry essay, although, or because, I had never drawn a pie. I had my own laden blueberry bushes if I wanted to draw the actual berries, but I was too busy eating and freezing them to find the time to draw them. Plus I wanted to add a bit of diversity to the book, and perhaps wanted a new excuse to visit North Hill. I e-mailed Wayne and suggested I draw a pie. Joe called soon thereafter and said, "Come for lunch at eleven tomorrow and Wayne will bake you a pie."

Lunch was fresh from the garden as expected, but a mere prelude to dessert. The pie was gorgeous. I was informed that Wayne had not followed Aretha Franklin's lattice shortcut—Joe would never have allowed it. After all the colorful stories I'd heard of friends and acquaintances from around the world, I was willing to accept that Wayne and the Queen of Soul had traded pointers on how best to weave a lattice piecrust, but it turns out that Wayne had watched her on a cooking show and she had almost persuaded him that he need not interweave the lattice strips. Joe overruled her.

After photographs were taken to satisfy my drawing plans, the pie was served on their lovely blue dishes, handmade and collected during a sabbatical in Denmark. As if taste alone was not enough to clean up my plate, I was always eager to admire the exquisite pottery and was glad conversation lingered after we finished eating. A writer from *Vermont Magazine* had joined us for lunch, and our discussion turned to Wayne's musings on whether or not he really felt a part of Vermont or was more grounded in a larger more cosmopolitan world. From everything he said, and more importantly from everything that lay outside the door in their magnificent garden, it was obvious what the answer was. He was a part of it all. Wayne and Joe's life—their plants, their friends, their stories—came from around the world, city and country alike. Nothing could separate him from Vermont, and nowhere else could have contained and nurtured the magnificence that is North Hill. Those of us fortunate enough to not only know Wayne and Joe but to live nearby, recognize the firmness of the foundation Vermont has provided but rejoice in all they have added with their broad minds and fabulous spirits.

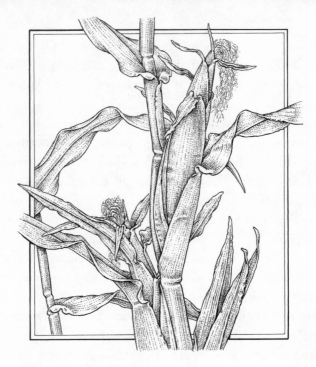

CORN

With deep pleasure we both remember the first ripening of the sweet corn in our grandparents' gardens. In Louisiana, for Wayne, this was in earliest summer. In Philadelphia, for Joe, with great horticultural skill at work, Granddad would serve sweet corn on the Fourth of July. In neither place was the season very long, six or eight weeks at best. In the South the crop was taken off by the blistering heat of high summer and in the North the shorter days and cooler nights of September marked the season's end. But in both our houses it was, for its time, almost all we ate.

When we lived in Boston, we both had work near enough the country, that is, Concord or Lexington, that a quick stop on a summer's afternoon at a local farm stand was a frequent oc-currence. And then, of course, we moved to the country. And it was there we learned about raccoons. Our first vegetable garden was a raggedy pants affair, weedy, without walls or paths, but still it produced plenteous food—broccoli, cauliflower, squash and, we thought, corn. We planted as Thalassa Cruso had taught us, in blocks rather than rows, and the corn bore heavily with promising tassels and, in time, great fat ears. But we weren't the only inhabitants of that Pepperell farm who kept watch on that garden. A groundhog had early on helped himself to much squash and cabbage, and so we shot him. But the raccoons were interested in only one crop, and they kept themselves hidden until it was just ripe for picking.

The morning that came was heartbreaking. The entire patch was trashed, canes broken, ears stripped but not fully eaten, just a bit taken from each and the rest lying useless on the ground.

That night they took a third of the crop, but we were determined to keep the rest. Our farm neighbors offered but two suggestions: to wait out the night with guns in hand and shoot what came, or to surround the path with electric fence wire. Since we neither much looked forward to a sleepless night or the murder of a simple, if clever beast whose sole crime was the need to eat, we went off to Agway for an electric charger and some fence wire. No harvest of corn would approach the cost of the charger, but that wasn't the point. It did work. The tracks of the coon stopped at the fence and he never returned. That year Joe's birthday, August 14, was a feast of corn. Wayne made corn pudding, the first Joe had tasted, and succotash and, of course, corn on the cob. Eating as we do, only what's in season, we gorged on, or, to put it more poetically, we celebrated corn. Corn was part of every meal for two months as it is here in Vermont in season. It is never eaten in any form out of season. And though corn, like so many vegetables, is easily frozen, we eschew that practice so we can hold on to that delightful sense of gift when any crop time comes round.

Corn is a crop of great interest—to economists, to farmers, to commodity traders, and to scholars. Treasured by Native

Americans and invested with great spiritual significance, it has in Anglo culture become a central commodity crop, used ubiquitously in the food industry, traded and speculated on, planted over hundreds of thousands of acres at tremendous ecological cost. These large economic and historic issues with corn have been extensively written about, most famously in Michael Pollan's *The Omnivore's Dilemma* and earlier in Betty Fussell's *Story of Corn*. But our concerns are more self-interested. We are concerned with what corn tastes best and grows well in our garden. Taste, of course, is a question of personal preference. And our preference is for the corn of our childhoods.

Country lore has always counseled that corn must be cooked as soon as possible after picking. Corn sugar converts quickly to starch, hence the admonishment to put the pot of water to boil before walking to the garden. Hybridizers have over the last few decades bred for corn that would more slowly convert sugar to starch and also to increase the sugar content of the kernels. Most corn bought today at markets, super or farm, is of this sugar-enhanced sort. Super sweet or triple sweet. These corns remain sweet long after they are picked and so are preferred by marketers. We detest them. Though they are sweet even days after picking, that is all they are. The flavor of corn is swamped by sweetness. They are to corn as Miracle Whip is to whipped cream.

So we grow only open-pollinated old-fashioned sweet corn. These are chewier than modern hybrids. The kernels stick to one's teeth and have a taste we remember. Golden Bantam, introduced in 1902, is perhaps our favorite. Early to mature, its smallish ears are filled with gold kernels of intense flavor. We grew it many years ago in Pepperell and grow it still. We also grow Stowell's Evergreen, introduced fifty-four years earlier than Golden Bantam, in 1848. This variety we have recently sought out through the Seed Savers Exchange, increasingly the source of much of our vegetable seed. The Seed Savers Exchange, founded in 1975, is devoted to the preservation of old open-pollinated varieties of vegetables no longer commercially available. Whatever the commercial liabilities of these old forms, they are almost always more flavorful than modern hybrids. And the deepest reward of a country life is that its deliberate embrace of a small conserving ethic opens one to the rhythms, values, habits, and flavors of another time.

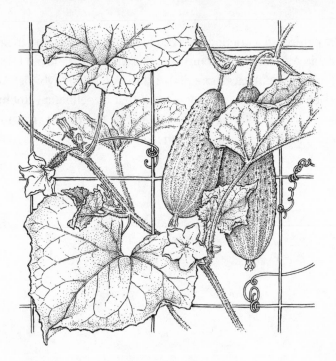

CUCUMBERS

These are not really interesting. Except in two forms. Our son, who is Greek, has taught us to love tzatziki, and that is good. So also are the funny English cucumber sandwiches, startlingly bland but somehow comforting.

We grow a beautiful lemon cucumber, bright yellow, a little pithy, but full of flavor. And old, from the eighteenth century. Thomas Jefferson grew it. And Washington and Madison. That alone is reason enough to cultivate it. And it always startles guests. What is this, they ask, so odd-looking a thing.

And we grow a wonderful little green one from Italy, Piccolo di Parigi, meant for pickling but delicious just to eat, crisp, flavorful, excellent. Our dear friend just down the road, Faith Sprague, now gone, was a true country woman born on this hill and deeply versed in country ways. We took her one summer's day a basket of Piccolo di Parigi. From it she made the most extraordinary pickles, so thin one could read the paper through them, at once both sour and sweet. She called them Confederate, though we don't know why, for Faith had never been down there and knew no Southerners—but us. They were the finest pickles we have ever tasted and now that Faith is dead we will never taste their like.

We grow cucumbers in an artful fashion. We make a frame of tall bamboo canes and then we weave a lattice of hemp into small little squares. It is beautiful from the first and more so as the vines embrace it. This is for the health of the vines, which must have air about them and no contact with the humid ground. And it makes them easy to observe and pick. Gardening should always be artful, be it the rose garden, the primrose garden, or the vegetable. Finding ways of beautifully engendering one's crops is what a true gardener does.

PEAS

Of this we cannot write better, and so this chapter is taken from *Our Life in Gardens*.

No one can say that a gardening life is rich in leisured holidays, but a gardener's rewards are festivals, big and small, though we make little distinction there, for they are all wonderful. There are other activities in which effort and labor are so certainly followed by achievement and celebration, and anyone who takes an active hand in shaping life must know equal causes for joy. We know only our life, which is largely one of gardening. So bulbs planted with raw fingers in October flower in April, their abundance in rewarding proportion to the effort of five months before. A richness of roses comes fast on the heel of the painful

pruning and staking, feeding and spraying that roses both require and so abundantly reward. And for all our bruised knees
and chapped fingers and sunburnt noses, we feel lucky. For
whereas even children have only their birthday and Christmas,
Halloween and Easter, and the End of School mostly to antici-
pate, we can look forward to a host of special events, the season
of snowdrops, and then of daffodils, then of magnolias and
Stewartias, and after that of lilacs and roses, poppies, asters, col-
chicum, autumn crocus, and snow.

Our years are rich, but though we are generally aware of our
wealth, it is the vegetable garden that most makes us clip our
coupons and chuckle at our dividends. We start with Egyptian
onions, our earliest crop, which may be harvested and sautéed as
scallions in early April when the snow is barely gone. Fine spring
lettuces and radishes overlap them, and then green garlic and
asparagus, and then strawberries and raspberries, blueberries
and currants, and then we are at sea with high summer, the great
bark of which is corn and tomatoes, all one wants in that season
to eat.

A few crops and the festivals that attend their maturity are
no trouble at all. Squash is like that. You put the seed in the
ground, and a few short weeks later, you harvest the young fruits.
Tomatoes require more effort, for they must be trained into cor-
dons on bamboo stakes, and suckered and tied in, and the pests
that get them in the end—wilts and mosaics and fungus—must
be constantly fought with organic sprays, copper sulfate for
choice. Cucumber vines must be twiddled up on strings, lest the
vines crab along the ground, making the harvest a process of
wading through a surf of sticky green leaves. Most vegetable crops
are labor-intensive, really, but it is by the sweat of one's brow that
one eats, and that is a good thing always to remember.

No crop is more labor-intensive than peas, and perhaps none
is more treasured here. Effort may well equal appreciation in
many human activities, and we would argue as much. What

those who do not garden never seem to understand, however, is that the effort exists in one place (and brings its own pleasures), and the appreciation of its reward is in quite another. Peas are a lot of work, for the ground must be prepared early, heavily enriched with good well-rotted poultry-yard compost, and made mellow with powdered lime. The work doesn't stop there, for once the peas are sown in mid-April, cages must be constructed above the drills to support the vines. Peas are climbing plants that attach themselves by tendrils to whatever will boost them up into the light. In the wild, any old bush or twig will do, for their interest is entirely in reproducing, and they often form hopeless tangles that matter little to their essential purpose, though it matters greatly to anyone bent on harvesting their edible seeds.

For the support of peas we have two methods, depending on their anticipated height. Tall-growing varieties, such as Alderman (also wonderfully named Tall Telephone), may reach as much as seven feet, taller in fact than the eight-foot bamboo poles we get from A. M. Leonard, a foot of which must be inserted into the ground to make the long two-sided structures on which the vines are trained. A row of poles is set four feet from one another, and a second row is set exactly opposite the first, at approximately three feet apart, row from row. The poles are then crossed at the top to form an X, and lashed to a ridgepole down the center. A second set of poles is tied along the length of this structure at near ground level, and to both sides we attach lengths of black plastic bird netting. Generally, we plant tall peas in long rows of about twenty feet in length, so a good half of a day's work is involved simply in constructing the structures, which will then be disassembled after the pea crop is finished and the last over-ripe pods have been gathered for Old Pea Soup. It is a lot of fun, and the great nineteenth-century gardener William Robinson did it for his sweet peas, which yielded nothing for the table but only beautiful flowers.

Even more entertaining is the construction of supports for lower-growing peas, often called bush peas, though we have found there is no such thing, since all peas scramble and their wayward habits irritate both gardener and cook, often one and the same. The lower-growing sorts include some of the very best and most flavorful peas one can grow, the famous petits pois of France. For them we use a different staking method, one that carries a glimpse of antique gardening the second it is put up.

Many willows grow throughout our garden. Many of them are pollarded in spring, their last year's growth cut into four- or five-foot lengths and carefully bundled up with twine from hay bales fed to the cows all winter long and hung on a forest branch. The willows are really grown for their own beauty, for the vivid egg-yolk yellow of *Salix alba* "Vitellina," the orange of *S. alba* "Chermesina," the scarlet of *Cornus sanguinea* "Winter Fire," or the dusty silver leaves of *S. alba* "Sericea." But the prunings are carefully saved as supports for the choicest peas we grow, not our main crop, certainly, for petits pois are quite frankly petit, each one hardly the size of a peppercorn. Still they are worth this trouble, which begins in early April and does not end until they are shelled in July.

Harvested willow twigs are inserted on either side of a rather wide row, with a hand-width trench down its middle, into which the tiny pea seed have been generously sown about twice their thickness deep, as close almost, as the old gardeners used to say, "as peas in a pod." (Or at least almost that close, for you can overdo the advice even of the Old Ones.) The twiggy willow stems are then gathered together into little huts or domes spaced about two feet apart, their tops bundled and tied with the same baling twine the twigs came up to the garden in, and the tops clipped off neatly all at the same height. The effect would have been quite familiar to Marie Antoinette, who cosseted her peas and cooked them herself in a silver saucepan with her own butter.

Besides the trouble of constructing supports—which, as we have tried to indicate, is a pleasure in itself for us—the cultivation of peas has two problems. Just after they have sprouted, peas have a curious way of thrusting themselves out of the ground. There is a wonderful sonnet by Robert Frost, which alludes to this fact, called "Putting in the Seed":

> You come to fetch me from my work tonight
> When supper's on the table, and we'll see
> If I can leave off burying the white
> Soft petals fallen from the apple tree
> (Soft petals, yes, but not so barren quite,
> Mingled with these, smooth bean and wrinkled pea),
> And go along with you ere you lose sight
> Of what you came for and become like me,
> Slave to a springtime passion for the earth.
> How love burns through the Putting in the Seed
> On through the watching for that early birth
> When, just as the soil tarnishes with weed,
> The sturdy seedling with arched body comes
> Shouldering its way and shedding the earth crumbs.

Pea seed must therefore be very firmly planted, and perhaps nothing is better than a foot newly naked to the warmth of spring and the feel of the living earth. But a gentler touch is required when the "sturdy seedling with arched body comes," for then earth from the side of the trench should be gently sprinkled over its head until it can catch root and grow. The other great problem is crows, mischievous, heavy-thinking, clever birds that know when a pea shoot is at its most succulent, most ready to be snatched from ground and gobbled up. But our staking methods foil them, since both methods look as if they could snare a bird, even a very big one.

Peas are beautiful even as tiny shoots, and their beauty increases steadily as they develop into little vines, clinging by tendrils to their supports. Soon mothlike flowers appear, snow white and never very numerous, each producing its tiny pod that develops into a plumpness the gardener recognizes as ready. Actually, the first ones are eaten straight from the vine, without the grace of even a splash of water, hot or otherwise, but soon there is a flood of peas, throughout July and even into August.

Everyone works for peas. They must be picked just at youthful maturity, when the pods are plump but not bursting at the seams, nicely filled out but still fresh with flavor. If the pods are yellowed or speckled or translucent, the peas inside are dense with starch and stolid, fit only for soup.

But when they are at prime, the last joyful work of peas can begin, the shelling of them late in the day, usually at the kitchen table or even before a fire if the evening is cool, as it is in July, usually, in Vermont. As green as anything on earth, the fresh peas are shelled into bowls and the pods tossed into baskets on the floor, a prize for the pigs, who fortunately do not discriminate between pea and pod.

It is interesting that all the great cookbooks we know have very few recipes for peas, and many lament the fact that there are never enough peas to do much with. That is, as it happens, not our problem, though we still cannot improve on the simplest of all recipes for peas, which is to plunge them into briskly boiling water for two or three minutes, drain them, and toss them with an appropriate amount of fresh butter. You could skip the butter. For that matter, you could skip the boiling water.

PEPPERS

We were, for many years, simply not very interested in peppers. Our house cuisine was largely English and French, and peppers play but a small role in these traditions. And, of course, peppers grow poorly in the wet, cool summers typical of Vermont. But that has all changed. Our preferences at table have shifted toward Mediterranean food, Greek, Spanish, and chiefly Italian. And the climate has shifted. Our summers are, while not drier, much warmer and the season is markedly longer.

The other evening we had dinner, as we often do, with our friend Beatrice at her marvelous Roman restaurant, Il Bagatto, on Second Street in the East Village. Bea is a purist. She cooks Roman food by completely traditional methods, the way her mother did. There is a Roman way and a wrong way. Each day there arrives from Rome a shipment of fresh produce—puntarelle, artichokes, radicchio, Castelfranco, and peppers. So the other evening, to be served a dish of blistered shishito peppers, small, sweet green peppers briefly turned in oil and dressed with salt, startled us. We ate them avidly, but to our query, "How Roman is this?" Bea simply shrugged. These were never on Mama's table.

Lately, peppers have become a passion here. John Thayer, one of our gardeners, last year trialed thirty different sorts. This year he intends fifty varieties in his garden on South Hill. At North Hill we will plant twenty varieties, eight sweet and twelve hot. Not that we would expect to consume in one summer the fruit of twelve rows of hot peppers. But hot peppers dry easily and can be used in that state throughout the winter. As we shall.

For sweet peppers we grow Corno Giallo, Yellow Bull's Horn; sweet with thin skin, it bears heavily in our new Vermont. It is bright gold in color. One sees it as soon as one opens the vegetable garden gate. We fry it and stuff it with beef and pork and feel always there is no more beautiful pepper in our garden. The Red Bull's Horn, Corno di Torro, is similarly sweet and showy, and we will grow it, too.

Of the bell peppers, our favorites are two orange varieties and two green. The Swiss Gourmet Orange is a large, heavily bearing bell, as sweet as all orange peppers seem to be. We will also grow Flavorburst, a modern hybrid, vigorous and disease-proof, also vibrant orange. But one must have green peppers, too, if only to note how much more flavorful those grown oneself are than those one buys in winter from Mexico or Guatemala. Aristotle and Revolution are both good new greens.

Gardening is, like so much else in life, fashion. Plants have their moment of wild popularity and then they settle back into an assumed place in our gardens. So, twenty years ago, we became fascinated with potatoes. We grew thirty sorts, cooked them all in every possible way, and then wrote a four-thousand-word article on them for *Horticulture* magazine. Till then most markets offered only boiling potatoes and russets from Idaho. Two years later, Yukon Gold and fingerlings and blue-fleshed purples were in every supermarket in America. So it is now with hot peppers. Jack Manix at Walker Farm in Dummerston tells us that last season he could not nearly meet the demand for hot, sometimes very hot, pepper plants. And though we have always been prideful of being ahead of the curve, we missed it this time, for the world has preceded us. We have a lot of catching up to do.

Of course we will grow shishitos, which are more mild than hot. Their sweetness is as notable. And begin Padron, too, for its small, mild, very sweet little peppers with an occasionally very hot one. Eat a plate of Padrons and you are eating Russian roulette. Truly hot peppers are rated for heat on the Scoville scale, a measure of the amount of capsaicin in its tissues and seeds. Czech Black, a jet-black pepper, is rated at 100,000 Scoville units. This is hot as, in another sense, the plant, which has purple flowers and leaves veined in purple.

Last season we fell in love with Bird Hots, peppers first grown in America by Thomas Jefferson. They make dozens of little round peppers carried erect on tall plants. Birds love them, hence the name. They, too, are rated at about 100,000 Scoville units.

Very much hotter is Peperoncini Bacio di Satana, Satan's Kiss. It is not ill named. Like most hot peppers, it forms fine *ristras* on garlands dried for winter use.

The hottest peppers in our garden this year will be Bhut Jolokia, from Thailand, rated at a life-endangering 1,000,000 Scoville units. This pepper must always be handled with gloves and eye protection. A little of this pepper is quite enough.

We have ordered two other specialty peppers this year for North Hill. Holy Mole is obviously Mexican, an essential part of mole sauce. One of our first meals together forty years ago was chicken mole, which we both remember still. It has been followed by many throughout our lives. And we must also grow a pepper for goulash. Paprika Alana forms round, slightly flattened red balls that are both peppery and sweet. It can easily be ground when dry for paprika.

One of gardening's continuing joys is the rebirth of enthusiasm. Just when everything seems to have been grown, a whole new world of plants and tastes appears. In what other part of human life is this true?

Peperoni con Acciughe, Olive Nere, e Capperi
(Peppers with Anchovies, Black Olives, and Capers)

5 tablespoons extra-virgin olive oil
5 garlic cloves cut in half (if you have good tasty garlic,
     only use 3 cloves)
4 anchovy fillets, chopped
½ cup pitted Gaeta or Kalamata olives
2 tablespoons capers
4 large peppers any color you want, mix it up, cut into
     ⅛-inch slices
2 pinches spicy red crushed chili pepper (peperoncino)
Sea salt to taste (anchovies, olives, and capers are all
     salty)

In a large sauté pan over medium heat, sauté the garlic in the olive oil. When the garlic starts coloring, add the anchovies, letting them melt in the oil, then the olives and the capers, and cook for 3 minutes. Add the peppers and peperoncino, stir until all the ingredients are blended together. Cover.

Come back to the pan and give it a stir every once in a while. If the dish looks dry, add a little water. Once the peppers are cooked through and glazed, taste to see if salt is needed, then remove the pan from the fire and let it cool.

I like to prepare this dish a day in advance, and I also like to roast and peel the peppers for a lighter dish.

SERVES 4–6

From the kitchen of Beatrice Tosti di Valminuta

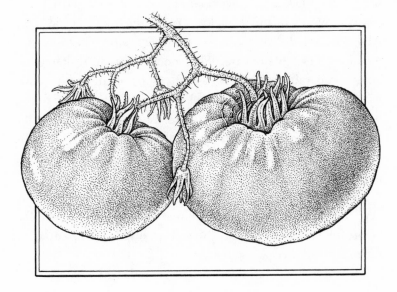

TOMATOES

Fruit. Not vegetable. And to eat a fine one in August, warmed by the sun, so apparent. As fine as any apricot or plum.

This is perhaps the most debased of all our foods. Breeders have labored for decades to make a fruit without taste. They wanted one that is red, unblemished, and tough skinned so it ships easily, fruiting in winter in Florida or California or in greenhouses.

But ironically, the richness of this fruit has in the last twenty years also been richly restored. The heirlooms, cultivars grown by our grandparents, almost extinct, have been returned to us. Their names themselves are infectious. Mortgage Lifter, Yellow Peach, Red Pear, Green Zebra, Brandywine. Each different in appearance, in flavor, in texture. So we should offer a few of the perhaps two thousand cultivars just to show how rich and varied a fruit the tomato is.

Some years ago while working in a garden in San Diego, we stumbled upon Chino, a legendary place. A modest farm stand, wooden, with a dirt parking lot, it offers the finest vegetables in America. Small savory carrots, strawberries of rich taste, and tomatoes. The tomatoes are all heirlooms, often difficult to grow but incomparable in taste. We bought many, ate most, but kept a few for seed. One of those was Yellow Peach. It is small and fuzzy, hence the name, and delicious. Most like a fruit. It is not for keeping, rotting after a week or so, but is the sweetest, most startling of its tribe. We like it best. We took one, disemboweled it, put the seeds on paper towels to dry, and in spring, sowed them. It came to live in Vermont and lives here still, the seed carefully kept from year to year. Amy Goldman, in her grand book, *The Heirloom Tomato*, says of it, "So soft, so luscious, so pleasing to the touch and eye." All so true.

Brandywine is utterly other. Huge, red, with smooth skin. Accustomed as we are to the large and largely tasteless modern tomatoes, Big Boy, et cetera, the taste of Brandywine is startling. For it has flavor, sweetness more than sharpness, but is deeply satisfying. This tomato has a rich history. Introduced in 1889, it has been valued ever since—for its flavor but also for its beauty. Of all the heirlooms, it was the least endangered, for gardeners have always cherished it. And it is in a way why this delectable plant has come back to us, for it stood in such contrast to the stuff of agribusiness and we all knew the difference and wondered what else we might have lost.

Another. Green Zebra. Not red. Beautiful, green skinned with lovely yellow stripes. It is delicious in an odd way, crisp, green, firm—again, a fruit. We think tomatoes are remarkable because they have such complexity, such a richness in variety, in taste, and in appearance, and in the garden in the way they grow. Some have the oddest leaves, great broad things rather like potatoes, to which they are cousins.

There are small ones, too, with ordinary leaves but like nothing ordinary you might find in markets, probably closer to their wild progenitor. Matt's Wild Cherry is new, introduced by Johnny's Selected Seeds, Albion, Maine, only in 1996. But to eat it is to find yourself transported to another age. The flavor is delectable and wild, almost too enchanting. And there are other small ones. The currants, for example. There are many: Red Currant, Sweet Pea Currant, Black Cherry, White Currant, Green Grape. They are small, and all the flavor seems so much more wonderful in so little a space.

There are so many. But let us close with one, Purple Calabash. It is our most precious. This tomato is so beautiful. Warted, folded, ribbed, wholly odd. And delicious. Like nothing anyone might buy at a Shaw's or a Gristedes. But isn't that what growing real food is all about? This is fine, finer, finest.

AFTERWORD

It was in late winter when I wrote the last of this book, our book. And how oddly each day Wayne had been with me, in his room as always, and me still going up the stairs to ask him to hear a paragraph or help me find a word. Not a fantasy but an easy conversation with a lifelong companion.

But the book done, he went away. I tried to lure him back. I cooked from the little cookbook *Now You Finally Got a Boyfriend* he had written for Fotios. I slept in his bed. I even appropriated some of his clothes. Each act was futile and lonely.

I stopped eating. I don't think I made that decision, I just stopped. And drinking anything other than wine. Friends tried to help. John cooked several nights, and I vomited up the food. I let the dandelion days pass by. And the fiddleheads. Still I functioned. I worked on other people's gardens but not my own.

I didn't even walk in it. Nor did I play the piano or even listen to music. Then one day at lunch with John, I collapsed. He rushed me, unconscious, to the hospital, assuming a heart attack. But it was simple exhaustion and complete dehydration. I was put in intensive care. A week later they let me go home, and for the first time I understood.

Just last Friday, my wonderful new psychiatrist, Robin, said I must live again by little steps. And so I hoed the vegetable garden and today I will plant parsley. And now begin to fashion a separate life, one I never envisioned or wanted but I am fated to. As are we all.

Index